Hypergraphics'
Simplified User Guide for Microsoft ®
WINDOWS™ *3.0*

Richard Maran

Hypergraphics Inc.
Mississauga, Ontario, Canada

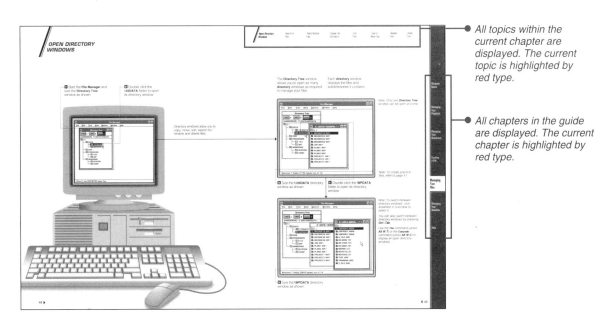

All topics within the current chapter are displayed. The current topic is highlighted by red type.

All chapters in the guide are displayed. The current chapter is highlighted by red type.

HOW TO USE THIS GUIDE

The table of contents is graphically represented on every right facing page. Quickly access the information you require by:

Finding the Chapter

While flipping through the pages of the guide, scan the right hand side of the page to locate the chapter you want.

Finding the Topic within the Chapter

Once you are within the desired chapter, scan the top right hand side of the pages to locate the topic you want. Flip to that highlighted page.

Hypergraphics'
Simplified User Guide for Microsoft ®
WINDOWS™ 3.0

Acknowledgements

Copyright ©   Hypergraphics Inc. 1991
             5755 Coopers Avenue
             Mississauga, Ontario
             Canada   L4Z 1R9

             "Screen Shots" © 1985-1990 Microsoft
             Corporation. Reprinted with permission
             from Microsoft Corporation.

Canadian Cataloguing in Publication Data

Maran, Richard
    Hypergraphics' simplified user guide for
Microsoft Windows 3.0

Includes index.
ISBN 0-9694290-3-7

1. Microsoft Windows (Computer programs).
I. Title.

QA76.76.W56M37 1991   005.4'3   C91-093144-5

Wholesale distribution:

Firefly Books Ltd.
250 Sparks Avenue
Willowdale, Ontario
Canada   M2H 2S4

Special thanks to Allan Watson of Microsoft Canada
Inc. and Richard Livesley of the Bank of Montreal for
their support and consultation.

To the dedicated staff at Hypergraphics Inc. and
HyperImage Inc., including Monica DeVries, Lynne
Hoppen, Jim C. Leung, Robert Maran, and Elizabeth
Seeto for their artistic contribution.

To Eric Feistmantl who was always there to solve my
technical and operational problems.

And finally to Maxine Maran for providing the
organizational skill to keep the project under control.

Trademark Acknowledgements

*Cover Design &
Graphics Consultant:*
Erich Volk

Art Direction:
Jim C. Leung

Production:
Monica DeVries
Jim C. Leung
Elizabeth Seeto

Linotronic L-300 Output:
HyperImage Inc.

Table of Contents

START WINDOWS

To start Microsoft® Windows™ 3.0 from MS-DOS, type **win** and then press **Enter**.

```
C:\> win_
```

ASSUMPTIONS

■ Windows 3.0 is installed on your hard disk in a subdirectory named \WINDOWS.

■ A mouse is used with Windows 3.0.

CONVENTIONS

If key names are separated by a plus (+), press and hold down the first key before pressing the second key (example: **Ctrl+Esc**).

If key names are separated by a comma (,) press and release the first key before pressing the second key (example: **Alt,F**).

WINDOWS

Windows allows you to increase your productivity and work more intuitively with the computer.

Windows can run multiple programs at the same time, help manage and organize your files, and copy data between applications.

Windows contains Program item icons. These icons represent programs.

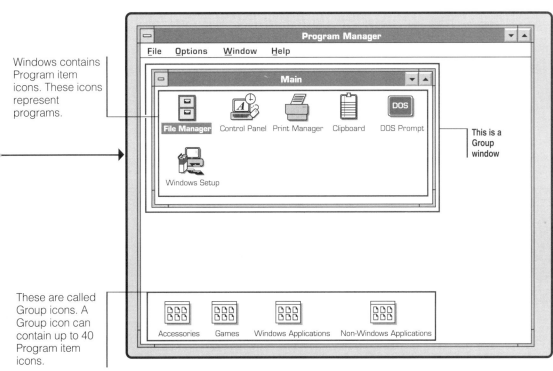

The entire computer screen is called the desktop. Multiple windows can be displayed on the desktop.

This is a Group window

These are called Group icons. A Group icon can contain up to 40 Program item icons.

Note: The terms "program" and "application" are used interchangeably.

Windows 3.0 includes built-in intelligence. After you type **win** to start the program, it checks your computer's hardware and memory and then starts Windows in the appropriate mode.

Note: The Group icons **Windows Applications** and **Non-Windows Applications** may or may not appear on the desktop, depending on the applications installed during Setup.

Windows Basics

Managing Your Programs

Managing Your Directories

Creating a File

Managing Your Files

Managing Your Diskettes

Help

WINDOWS THREE OPERATING MODES

REAL MODE

The Real Mode starts when the computer contains less than 1 megabyte of memory.

STANDARD MODE

The Standard Mode starts when the computer is an 80286 or 80386 machine and contains 1 megabyte or more of memory.

386 ENHANCED MODE

The 386 Enhanced Mode starts when the computer is an 80386 (or higher) machine and contains 2 megabytes or more of memory.

MOVE AND ARRANGE ICONS // MOVE A WINDOW

MOVE AN ICON

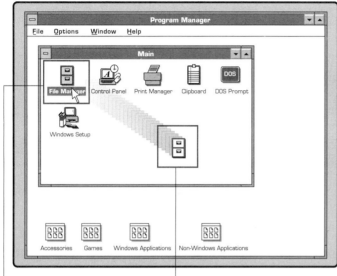 

1 Move the mouse ⬚ over an icon (example: **File Manager**). Click the left button and hold it down.

2 Still holding down the button, drag the icon to where you want it positioned in the window.

3 Release the button and the icon stays at its new position.

Note: All icons on the desktop can be moved this way.

MOVE A WINDOW

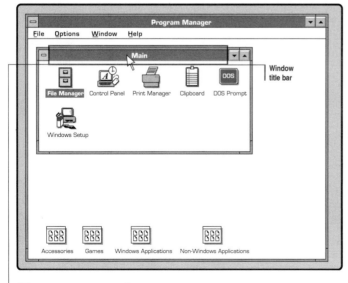 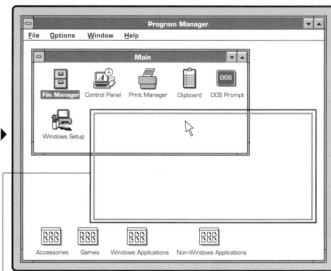

1 Move the mouse ⬚ over any part of the **Window title bar**. Click the left button and hold it down.

2 Still holding down the button, drag the window to where you want it positioned.

*Note: You cannot move the **Main** window outside the **Program Manager's** window.*

4 ▶

ARRANGE ICONS

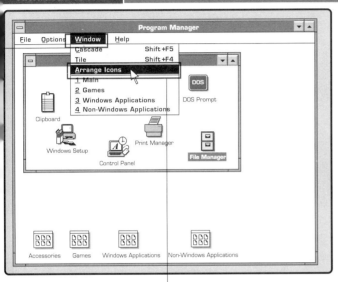

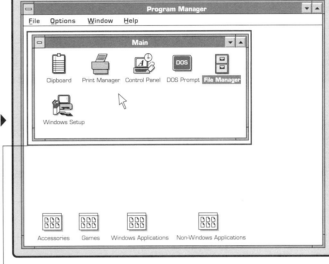

Windows Basics

Managing Your Programs

Managing Your Directories

Creating a File

Managing Your Files

Managing Your Diskettes

Help

1 To arrange icons in the **Main** window, move the mouse over **Window** and click the left button. Its menu appears.

Note: To cancel a menu, press Esc.

2 Move the mouse over **Arrange Icons** and click the left button.

☞ **Shortcut:**
Press **Alt**,**W**,**A**.

■ All the icons in the window are displayed in an orderly fashion.

KEYBOARD SHORTCUT TO SELECT MENU COMMANDS

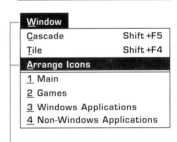

■ To select a menu command (example: **Arrange Icons**), press **Alt**,**W**,**A**.

W is the underlined letter for the **W**indow menu and **A** is the underlined letter for the **A**rrange Icons command.

Note: Windows commands are not case sensitive. You can press Alt,W,A or Alt,w,a.

3 Release the button and the **Main** window jumps to its new position.

Note: If you press Esc before releasing the button, the move is cancelled.

CHANGE A WINDOW'S SIZE

HORIZONTALLY

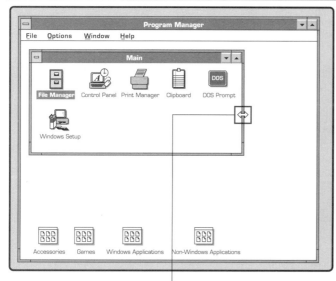

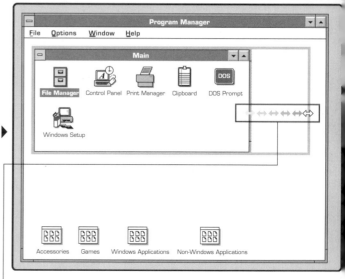

The ability to size each window independently is very useful when working with multiple windows on the desktop.

1 Move the mouse ▷ to the right edge of the window and it turns into ⇔.

2 Click and hold down the left button as you drag the edge of the window to the desired size.

HORIZONTALLY AND VERTICALLY AT THE SAME TIME

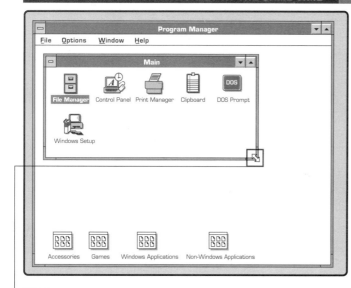

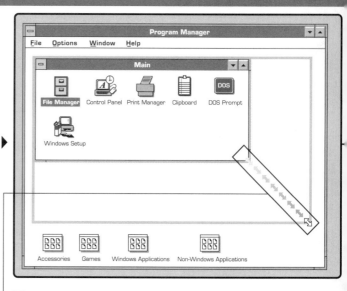

1 Move the mouse ▷ to the bottom right edge of the window and it turns into ⬉.

2 Click and hold down the left button as you drag the edge of the window to the desired size.

VERTICALLY

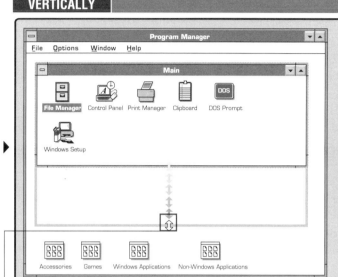

3 Release the button and the window is resized.

*Note: If you press **Esc** before releasing the button, the resizing is cancelled.*

4 Use the same method to resize the window vertically (except drag the bottom edge of the window).

Note: You can change a window's size to make it larger or smaller from any side or any corner. To automatically rearrange Program item icons when you resize a window, refer to page 10.

3 Release the button and the window is resized.

*Note: If you press **Esc** before releasing the button, the resizing is cancelled.*

Windows Basics

Managing Your Programs

Managing Your Directories

Creating a File

Managing Your Files

Managing Your Diskettes

Help

MINIMIZE AND RESTORE ICONS // MAXIMIZE AND RESTORE A WINDOW

MINIMIZE ICONS

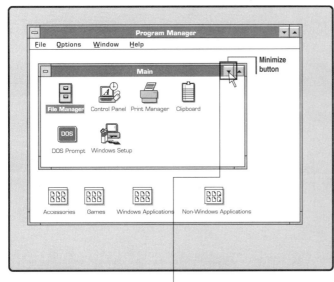

When you are finished working with a window, it can be turned into an icon to give you more working space on the desktop.

■ Resize the **Program Manager** and **Main** Group windows as shown above.

1 Move the mouse ⬦ over the **Main** window's **Minimize** button, and click the left button.

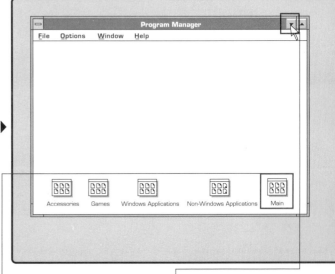

■ The **Main** window is reduced to an icon.

2 Move the mouse ⬦ over the **Program Manager** window's **Minimize** button, and click the left button.

MAXIMIZE A WINDOW

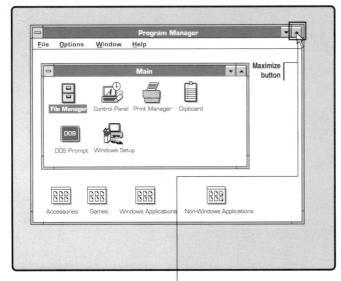

When working in a window, it can be enlarged to create a larger working area.

1 Move the mouse ⬦ over the **Program Manager** window's **Maximize** button, and click the left button.

■ The **Program Manager** window is enlarged to fill the entire space.

2 Move the mouse ⬦ over the **Restore** button, and click the left mouse button.

Windows Basics

Managing Your Programs

Managing Your Directories

Creating a File

Managing Your Files

Managing Your Diskettes

Help

RESTORE ICONS

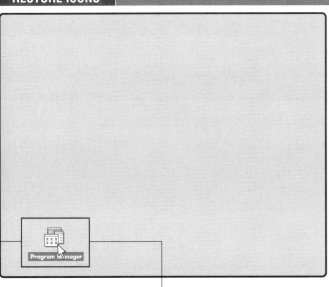

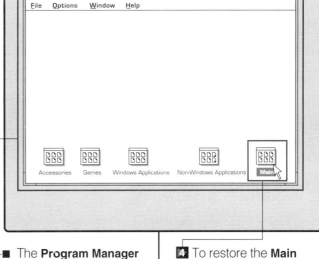

■ The **Program Manager** window is reduced to an icon.

3 To restore this icon to a window, move the mouse ⌖ over the icon and click the left button twice in quick succession.

■ The **Program Manager** window is restored.

4 To restore the **Main** window icon, move the mouse ⌖ over the icon and click the left button twice in quick succession.

■ The **Main** window is restored as displayed below.

RESTORE A WINDOW

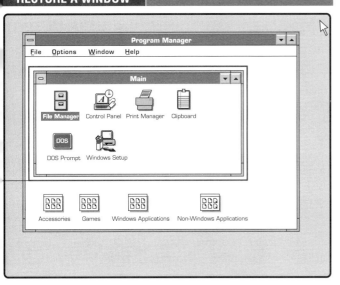

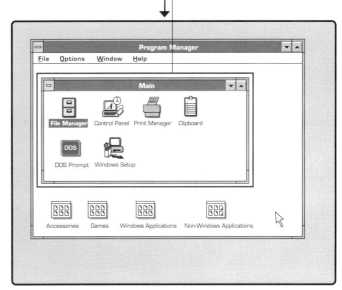

■ The **Program Manager** window is restored to its previous size.

*Note: The **Main** window can be enlarged to occupy the complete area within the **Program Manager** window and then be restored in the same way.*

AUTO ARRANGE ICONS

SELECT AUTO ARRANGE MODE

The Auto Arrange mode automatically rearranges Program item icons when you resize a window.

1 Move the mouse ⊾ over **Options** and click the left button. The Option menu appears.

2 Move the mouse ⊾ over **Auto Arrange** and click the left button to turn it **on**.

Note: If a checkmark (✔) is in front of Auto Arrange, it is already on.

☞ **Shortcut:**

Press **Alt,O,A**.

AUTO ARRANGE PROGRAM ITEM ICONS

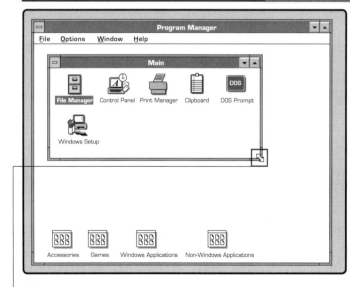

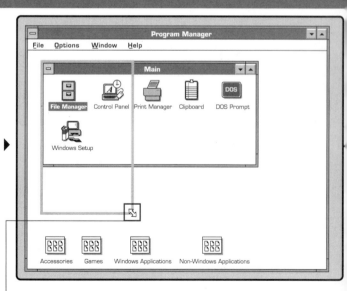

1 Move the mouse ⊾ to the right edge of the window and it changes to ⬂.

2 Click and hold down the left button as you drag the edge of the window to the desired size.

10 ▶

Windows Basics

Managing Your Programs

Managing Your Directories

Creating a File

Managing Your Files

Managing Your Diskettes

Help

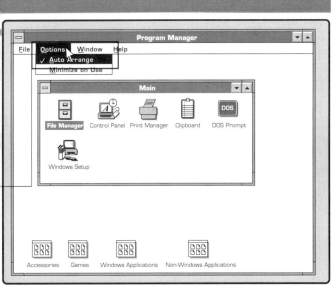

3 To check if the Auto Arrange mode is *on* or *off*, press **Alt**, **O**.

■ The checkmark (✓) in front of **Auto Arrange** indicates it is *on*.

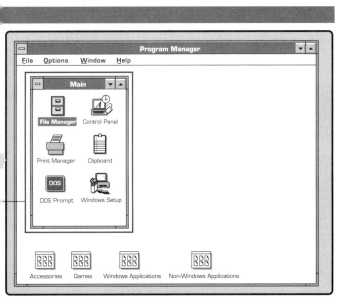

3 Release the button and the Program item icons are rearranged within the window.

EXIT
WINDOWS

EXIT WINDOWS USING THE MOUSE

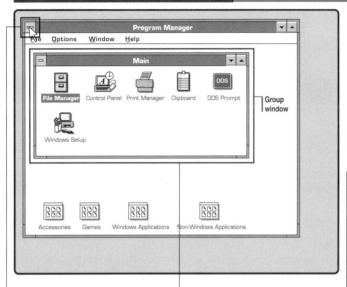

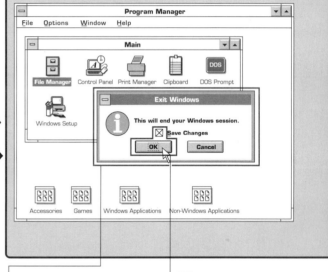

1 Move the mouse ⬚ over the **Control** box and click the left button twice in quick succession.

or

Use the keyboard method described below.

■ A Group window contains Program item icons. Each of these icons represents a program or application.

■ The **Exit Windows** dialog box appears.

Note: A dialog box requests or offers information to complete a task or function.

2 To exit Windows, move the mouse ⬚ over the **OK** button and click the left button or press **Enter**.

*Note: If the **Save Changes** box has a cross ⊠ through it, the current arrangement of Group windows and icons is saved.*

*If the **Save Changes** box is blank □, Group windows and icons revert to their preset or default settings.*

To toggle between □ and ⊠, move the mouse ⬚ over the box and click the left button.

MOUSE VS KEYBOARD

Operations in Windows 3.0 are performed using the mouse or keyboard.

For the rest of this guide, we have used either the mouse or the keyboard, depending on which was more efficient for the given operation. In some cases, we have shown both methods.

EXIT WINDOWS USING THE KEYBOARD

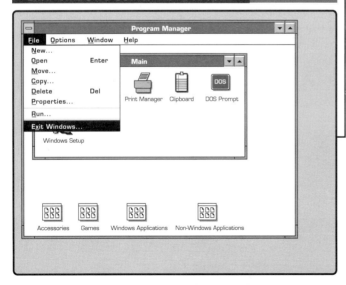

1 Press **Alt**, **F**, **X**.

☞ **Shortcut:**

Press **Alt+F4**.

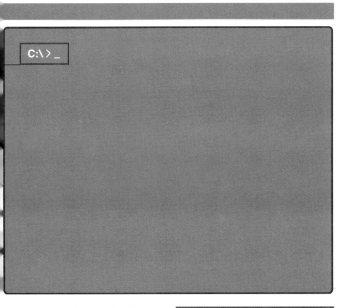

```
C:\> _
```

■ You are returned to the DOS prompt.

Caution

Always Exit Windows **before** turning off the computer.

DESCRIPTIVE SHORTCUTS

For the rest of this guide, the following shortcuts are used:

■ "Move the Mouse ▷ over **xx** and click the left button" becomes:

Click xx.

■ "Move the mouse ▷ over **xx** and click the left button twice in quick succession" becomes:

Double click xx.

■ "Move the mouse ▷ over **xx**. Click and hold down the left button as you drag **xx**" becomes:

Drag xx.

USING THE KEYBOARD IN A DIALOG BOX

Press **Tab** to move through the buttons and boxes of the dialog box. The button/box currently selected will have a dotted rectangle around its name.

After a box has been selected, press the **Space-bar** to toggle between **off** □ and **on** ⊠.

Press **Enter** to execute your selected choice(s).

Note: Windows contains a Help facility to provide you with more information on Dialog Box Keys.

While in the **Program Manager** window, press **Alt**,**H**,**K** and a Program Manager Help window appears. Move the ▷ pointer over Dialog Box Keys (the ▷ turns into a ⑬). Then click the left button and a **Dialog Box Keys** window appears.

Refer to page 74 for more information on how Help works.

Windows Basics

Managing Your Programs

Managing Your Directories

Creating a File

Managing Your Files

Managing Your Diskettes

Help

PROGRAM MANAGER

The Program Manager starts automatically after you type **win** at the C:\> prompt.

When you start up Windows the first time, the **Main** Group window opens.

To open another Group window (example: **Accessories**) double click its icon.

These icons represent programs. They are called Program item icons. Each program is started by double clicking its Program item icon.

Note: Group windows cannot be moved beyond the Program Manager window area.

Windows Basics

Managing Your Programs

Managing Your Directories

Creating a File

Managing Your Files

Managing Your Diskettes

Help

OPENING GROUP WINDOWS

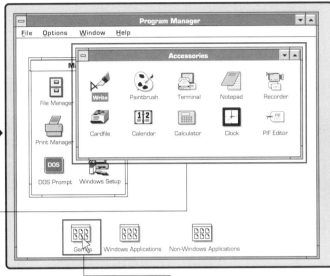

■ The **Accessories** Group window opens and becomes the current or active window.

2 To open the **Games** Group icon, double click its icon.

■ The **Games** Group icon opens and becomes the current window.

Note: The current window is identified by the highlighted title bar. Program Manager commands only work on the current window.

SWITCH BETWEEN GROUP WINDOWS

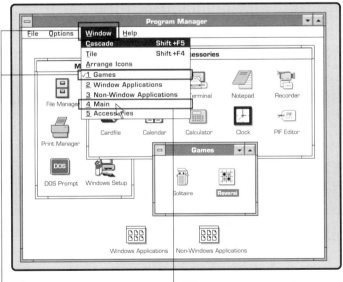

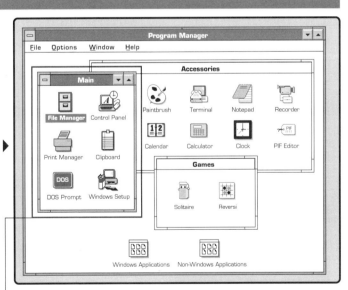

1 Press **Alt,W** and the **Window** menu appears. The (✓)in front of **Games** indicates its Group window is current.

2 To switch to another Group window (or make it the current window), click its name in the menu (example: **Main**).

■ The **Main** window becomes the current window.

Note: This feature is useful when the Group window you want is completely covered by another Group window.

☞ Shortcut:

Click in any window to make its window current.

◀ 15

CASCADE OR TILE GROUP WINDOWS

CASCADE OR TILE GROUP WINDOWS

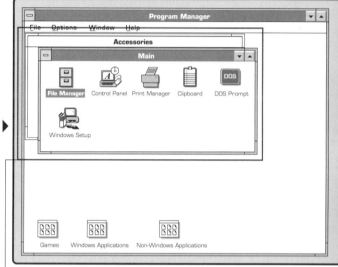

If several windows are open at the same time, some of them may be hidden. In this example, the Accessories window is hidden behind the Main window.

1 To **Cascade** the open Group windows, press **Alt,W,C**.

☞ **Shortcut:**
Press **Shift+F5**.

■ The **Main** and **Accessories** Group windows are cascaded.

2 To **Tile** the open Group windows, press **Alt,W,T**.

☞ **Shortcut:**
Press **Shift+F4**.

ADDING ANOTHER GROUP WINDOW

You may want to open other Group icons after selecting the Cascade or Tile command.

1 Double click the Group icon you want to open (example: **Games**).

■ The **Games** Group window appears.

2 To **Cascade** all three Group windows, press **Alt,W,C**.

*Program
Manager*

**Cascade or
Tile Group
Windows**

*Start Two or
More Applications*

*Using the
Task List*

*Using the
Run Command*

*Using the
DOS Prompt*

**Windows
Basics**

**Managing
Your
Programs**

**Managing
Your
Directories**

**Creating
a File**

**Managing
Your
Files**

**Managing
Your
Diskettes**

Help

■ The **Main** and **Accessories**
Group windows are tiled.

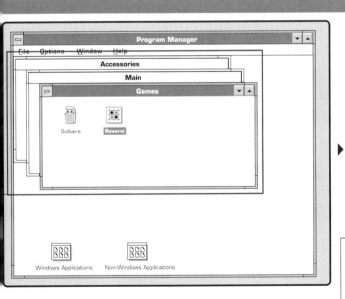

■ All three Group windows
are cascaded.

3 To **Tile** all three Group
windows, press **Alt**,**W**,**T**.

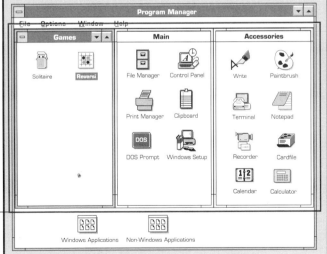

■ All three Group windows
are tiled.

START TWO OR MORE APPLICATIONS

START THE CALENDAR AND TERMINAL APPLICATONS

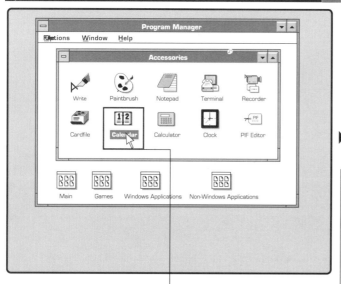 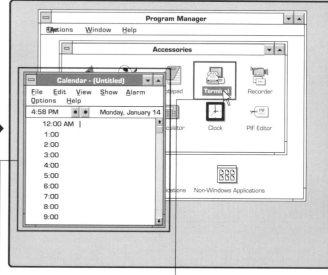

Windows can run two or more applications at the same time. For example, you can receive data from a modem while you are making appointments.

1 To start **Calendar**, double click its icon.

2 Resize the **Calendar** window as shown above.

3 To start **Terminal**, double click its icon.

Note: The Terminal program allows data exchange between computers. A modem is required.

SWITCH BETWEEN APPLICATIONS

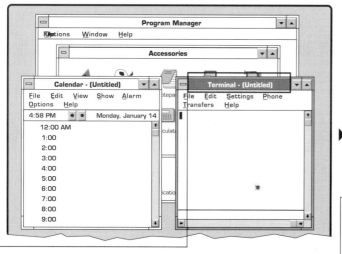 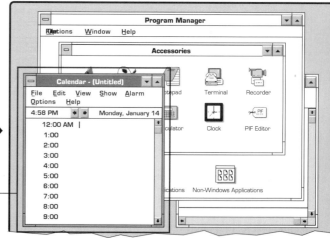

■ **Terminal** is the current or active application as indicated by its highlighted title bar.

*Note: The active application runs in the foreground. The other two applications, **Calendar** and **Program Manager**, run in the background.*

1 Press **Alt+Esc** and the **Calendar** window becomes active.

☞ **Shortcut:**

To make an application active, click in its window. This only works if the application is visible on the desktop.

Windows
Basics

Managing
Your
Programs

Managing
Your
Directories

Creating
a File

Managing
Your
Files

Managing
Your
Diskettes

Help

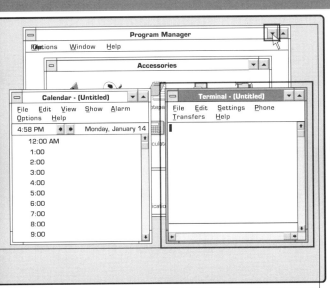

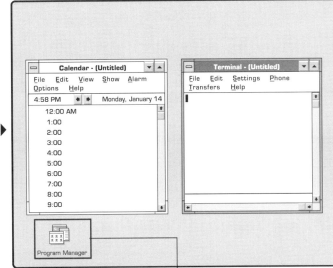

4 Resize the **Terminal** window as shown above.

Note: All three applications are running. However, only the window you are working in is active.

5 Reduce the **Program Manager** window to an icon by clicking its **Minimize** button.

*Note: All application windows can be reduced to icons by clicking their **Minimize** buttons.*

■ Both applications are running. **Terminal** is the active application.

■ The **Program Manager** window is easily accessed by double clicking its icon.

---

*Note: If more than three applications are open, continue pressing **Alt+Esc** to switch through the remaining applications.*

or

*Hold down **Alt** and press **Tab** until the desired window is active.*

2 Press **Alt+Esc** and the **Program Manager** window becomes active.

Note: You can only input or edit information in the active application window.

USING THE TASK LIST

SWITCH BETWEEN APPLICATIONS

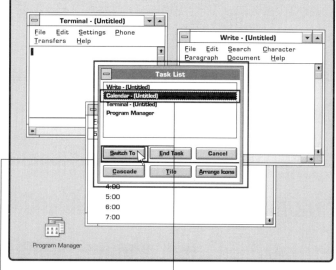

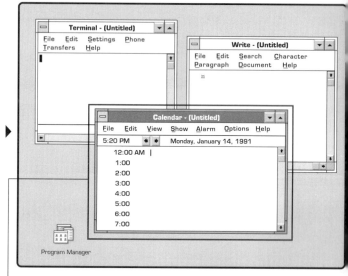

1 Start the **Terminal**, **Write** and **Calendar** applications by double clicking their icons. Then minimize the **Program Manager** window.

2 Press **Ctrl+Esc** and the **Task List** dialog box appears.

3 Click the application (example: **Calendar**) you would like to switch to.

4 Click the **Switch To** button or press **Alt+S**.

■ The **Calendar** window moves to the foreground and becomes the active window.

☞ Shortcut:

To open the **Task List**, double click anywhere on the desktop not covered by a window.

TILE OR CASCADE APPLICATION WINDOWS

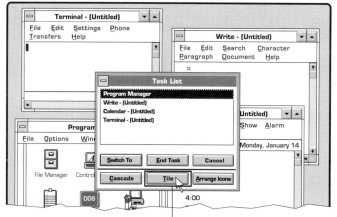

1 Press **Ctrl+Esc** and the **Task List** dialog box appears.

2 Click the **Tile** button or press **Alt+T**.

■ The four applications are tiled on the desktop.

*Note: Clicking the **Cascade** button displays all windows overlapped with their title bars showing.*

20 ▶

Windows Basics

Managing Your Programs

Managing Your Directories

Creating a File

Managing Your Files

Managing Your Diskettes

Help

ARRANGE APPLICATION ICONS

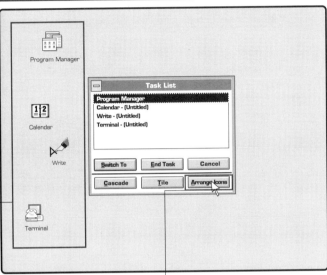

1 Reduce all applications to icons by clicking their **Minimize** buttons. Drag the icons to the locations shown above.

2 Press **Ctrl+Esc** and the **Task List** dialog box appears.

3 Click the **Arrange Icons** button or press **Alt+A**.

■ The application icons are arranged in order along the bottom of the desktop.

END TASK OR CLOSE AN APPLICATION

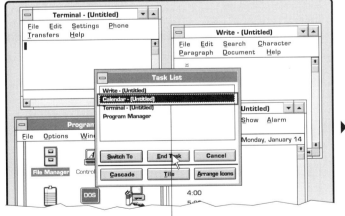

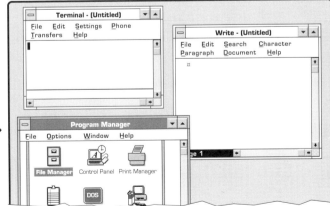

1 Press **Ctrl+Esc** and the **Task List** dialog box appears.

2 Select the application (example: **Calendar**) you want to close by clicking it.

3 Click the **End Task** button.

■ The **Calendar** application is closed.

*Note: If you select an application which is minimized on the desktop, the **Task List** will still close it.*

◀ 21

START APPLICATIONS USING THE RUN COMMAND

The Run command is used to start applications which run in the Windows environment.

Note: Adding a Windows program or application to a Group window is an advanced topic. Please refer to your Microsoft Windows User's Guide.

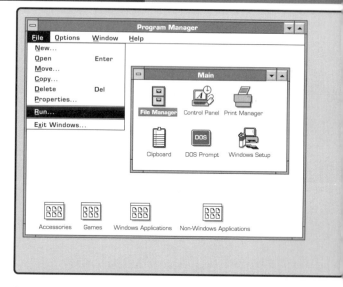

Suppose you want to open a program called Aldus PageMaker (program file is PM.EXE) located in drive C, subdirectory \PROGRAMS\PM.

1 To access the **Run** dialog box, press **Alt,F,R**.

START APPLICATIONS USING THE DOS PROMPT

The DOS Prompt icon is used to run non-Windows applications, while retaining your current window settings.

Note: DOS programs such as Norton utilities and CHKDSK/F that can modify the hard drive File Allocation Tables should not be run using the DOS Prompt icon.

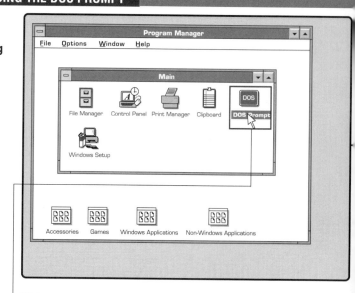

1 Double click the **DOS Prompt** icon to return to the DOS prompt C:\WINDOWS>.

Note: Refer to page 24 for information on how files and directories are specified.

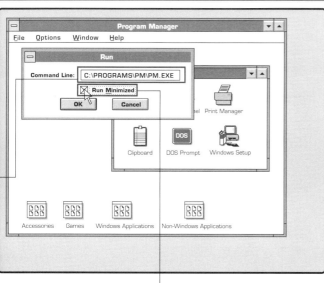

2 To start the PageMaker program, type **C:\PROGRAMS\PM\PM.EXE**, and then press **Enter**.

*Note: The **C:** can be eliminated if the current drive is C.*

3 Click the **Run Minimized** box ☐ to make it include an ☒, if you want the application reduced to an icon after it starts.

Note: PageMaker can then be opened quickly from the desktop by double clicking its Program item icon.

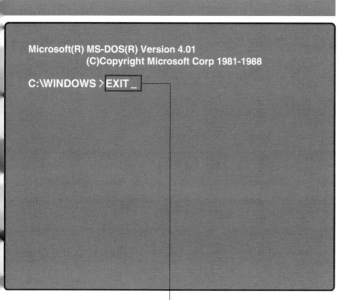

■ To use DOS, refer to Hypergraphics' MS-DOS Simplified User Guide.

2 Type **EXIT** and press **Enter** to return to Windows.

Windows
Basics

Managing
Your
Programs

Managing
Your
Directories

Creating
a File

Managing
Your
Files

Managing
Your
Diskettes

Help

FILES AND DIRECTORIES

HOW FILES ARE SPECIFIED

In an efficient and productive office environment, people create, edit, review and organize paper documents (example: letters, worksheets, reports, etc.). These documents are stored in folders, which in turn are placed in cabinets. To retrieve a specific document, you must identify it (by name) and by location (cabinet and folder).

Computers work the same way. After creating a document, it must be named and saved. During the save process, you must tell Windows the directory (folder) and drive (cabinet) the file is to reside in.

Note: A file is a document that has been given a name.

Windows lets you create a multilevel directory filing system to store and retrieve your files. The first level of this directory structure is called the root directory. From this directory other subdirectories can be created. A typical multilevel filing system is illustrated on the next page.

Note: The terms "directory" and "subdirectory" are used interchangeably. The "root directory" is the only "directory" that cannot be called a "subdirectory".

FILE SPECIFICATION

A file is specified by describing its pathname (drive and directory location within the computer), and its name (filename and extension).

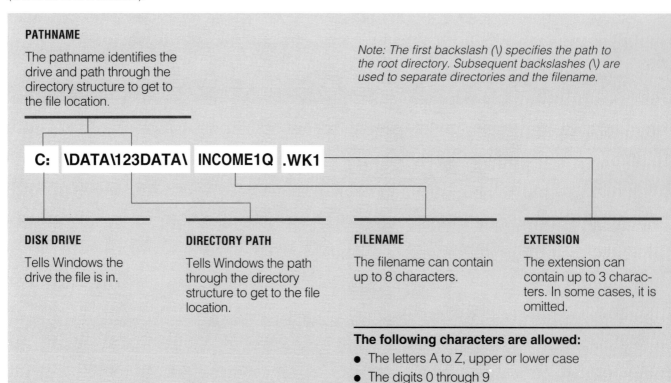

PATHNAME

The pathname identifies the drive and path through the directory structure to get to the file location.

Note: The first backslash (\) specifies the path to the root directory. Subsequent backslashes (\) are used to separate directories and the filename.

C: \DATA\123DATA\   INCOME1Q   .WK1

DISK DRIVE

Tells Windows the drive the file is in.

DIRECTORY PATH

Tells Windows the path through the directory structure to get to the file location.

FILENAME

The filename can contain up to 8 characters.

EXTENSION

The extension can contain up to 3 characters. In some cases, it is omitted.

The following characters are allowed:

- The letters A to Z, upper or lower case
- The digits 0 through 9
- $ # & @ ( ) - { } and _

USING DIRECTORIES TO ORGANIZE YOUR FILES

Directories can contain files and/or paths to other directories (example: the root directory has paths to four subdirectories).

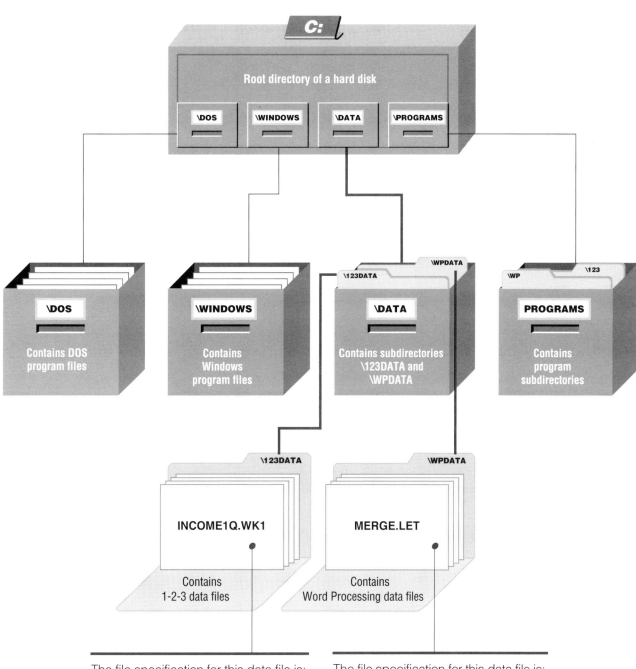

Root directory of a hard disk

\DOS   \WINDOWS   \DATA   \PROGRAMS

\DOS
Contains DOS program files

\WINDOWS
Contains Windows program files

\DATA
Contains subdirectories \123DATA and \WPDATA

PROGRAMS
Contains program subdirectories

\123DATA

INCOME1Q.WK1

Contains
1-2-3 data files

\WPDATA

MERGE.LET

Contains
Word Processing data files

The file specification for this data file is:

C:\DATA\123DATA\INCOME1Q.WK1

The file specification for this data file is:

C:\DATA\WPDATA\MERGE.LET

Windows Basics

Managing Your Programs

Managing Your Directories

Creating a File

Managing Your Files

Managing Your Diskettes

Help

FILE MANAGER

The File Manager helps you create, organize and manage your files and directories.

1 To start the **File Manager**, double click its icon.

Note: To keep the desktop uncluttered, you can minimize the current application (example: Program Manager) when you start or open a new application (example: File Manager).

MINIMIZE AN APPLICATION ON USE

Options
✓ **Auto Arrange**
✓ **Minimize on Use**

■ To check the status of **Minimize on Use**, press **Alt,O**.

■ If no checkmark is in front of **Minimize on Use**, it is **off**.

■ To turn it **on**, press **M**.

*Note: If a checkmark (✓) is already in front of **Minimize on Use**, it is **on**. Press **Esc** to retain the setting.*

Windows
Basics

Managing
Your
Programs

Managing
Your
Directories

Creating
a File

Managing
Your
Files

Managing
Your
Diskettes

Help

■ **DISK DRIVE ICONS**

Each floppy or hard drive on the computer is represented by an icon followed by its drive letter.

A – represents diskette drive A

C – represents hard drive C

The highlighted icon (**drive C**) is the current drive.

■ **DIRECTORY ICONS**

Each directory is represented by a folder.

The directory folders are sorted alphabetically in ascending order.

If a (**+**) sign is displayed on a directory folder, it contains subdirectories. If a (**–**) sign is displayed on a directory folder, its subdirectories are displayed beneath it.

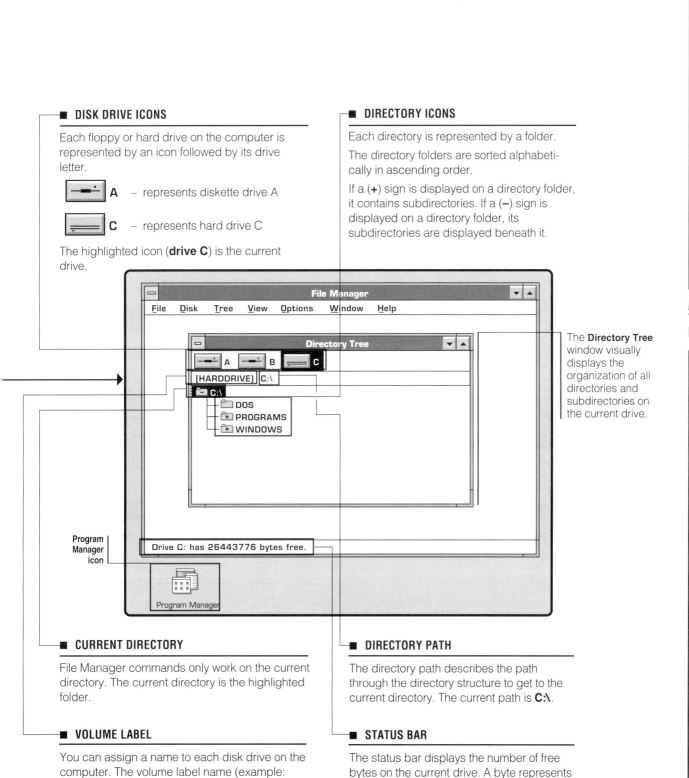

The **Directory Tree** window visually displays the organization of all directories and subdirectories on the current drive.

Program Manager icon

■ **CURRENT DIRECTORY**

File Manager commands only work on the current directory. The current directory is the highlighted folder.

■ **VOLUME LABEL**

You can assign a name to each disk drive on the computer. The volume label name (example: **HARDDRIVE**) appears within the **[ ]** brackets. Naming the disk drive is optional.

■ **DIRECTORY PATH**

The directory path describes the path through the directory structure to get to the current directory. The current path is **C:**.

■ **STATUS BAR**

The status bar displays the number of free bytes on the current drive. A byte represents one character.

CHANGE DISK DRIVES

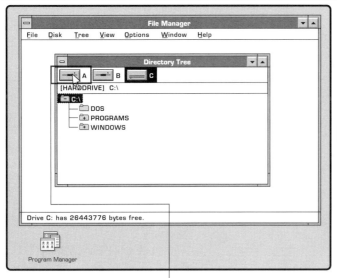

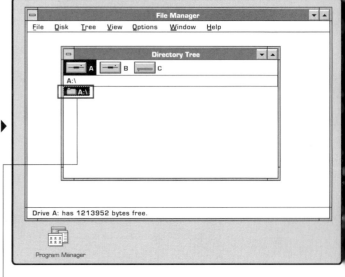

This screen displays the Directory Tree of the current disk drive. In this example, drive C is the current disk drive. It is easily identified by its highlighted icon and drive letter.

◄■ To change to another drive (example: **drive A**), click its icon.

> ☞ **Shortcut:**
>
> To change to drive A, press **Ctrl+A**.
>
> To change to drive B, press **Ctrl+B**.

■ The **Directory Tree** window displays the directory structure of the diskette in **drive A**.

Note: In this example, the diskette in drive A contains no subdirectories or data because it is a recently formatted diskette.

To learn how to format a diskette, refer to page 70.

CHANGE DIRECTORIES

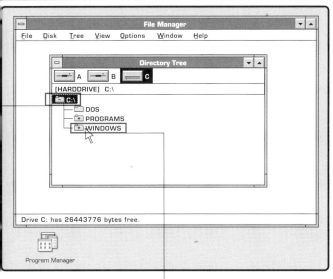

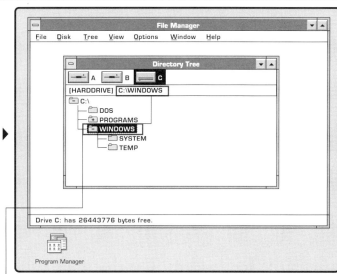

■ The current directory in the window is identified by the dotted line around its highlighted folder and name (example: **C:**).

 To change to another directory (example: **Windows**), click on its folder.

■ The current directory is changed to the **\Windows** directory.

*Note: The **\Windows** directory displays its subdirectories **\System** and **\Temp**.*

KEYBOARD SHORTCUTS

Press	Resulting action
↑ or ↓	Move up or down one directory
Home	Move to the root directory
End	Move to the last directory
Page Up	Move one directory window up from the current directory
Page Dn	Move one directory window down from the current directory
Type the first letter of the directory name	Move to the directory starting with that letter

USING THE NUMERIC KEYPAD

To use the numeric keypad's arrows, PgUp, PgDn, Home and End keys, **NumLock** must be *off*.

If the **NumLock** status light is *on*, press **NumLock** to turn it *off*.

Windows Basics

Managing Your Programs

Managing Your Directories

Creating a File

Managing Your Files

Managing Your Diskettes

Help

◀ 29

CREATE DIRECTORIES

All examples in this guide are based on the directory structure illustrated below:

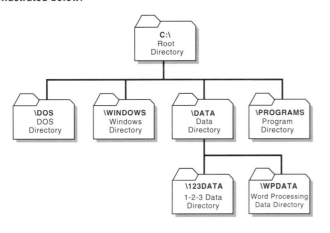

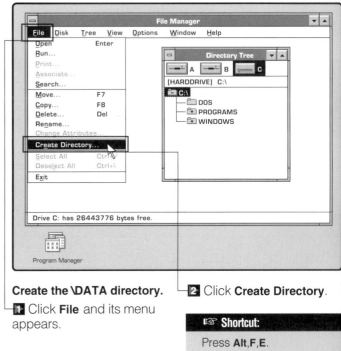

Create the \DATA directory.

1 Click **File** and its menu appears.

2 Click **Create Directory**.

☞ Shortcut:

Press **Alt,F,E**.

CREATE THE \123DATA AND \WPDATA DIRECTORIES

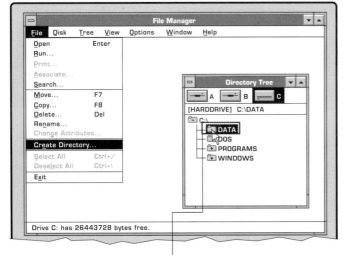

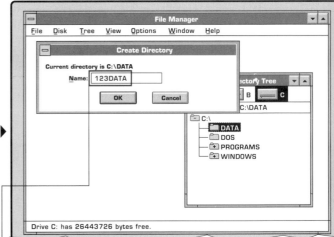

Create the \123DATA and \WPDATA directories one level below the \DATA directory.

1 Click the **DATA** folder to change it to the current directory.

2 To create a new directory, press **Alt,F,E**.

3 Type in the name of the new directory (example: **123DATA**) and then press **Enter**.

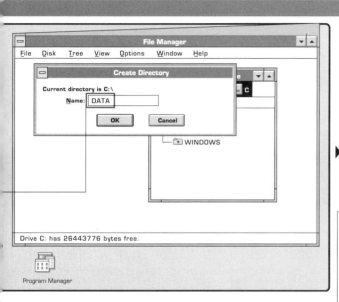

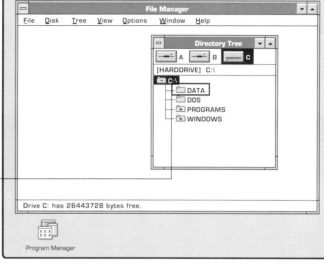

3 Type in the name of the new directory (example: **DATA**) and then press **Enter**.

Note: New directories are created one level below the current directory. In this example, the current directory is C:\.

■ The new **\DATA** directory is displayed.

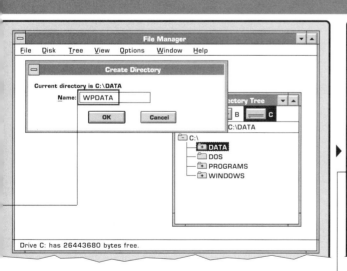

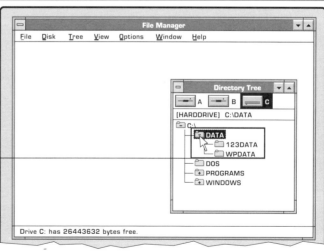

4 Repeat step **2**. Type in the name of the new directory (example: **WPDATA**) and then press **Enter**.

5 Click the **DATA** folder and the newly created subdirectories **\123DATA** and **\WPDATA** are displayed.

Windows Basics

Managing Your Programs

Managing Your Directories

Creating a File

Managing Your Files

Managing Your Diskettes

Help

EXPAND OR COLLAPSE DIRECTORY LEVELS

EXPAND ONE LEVEL OF A DIRECTORY

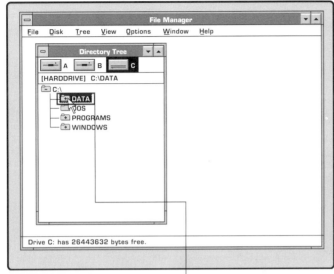 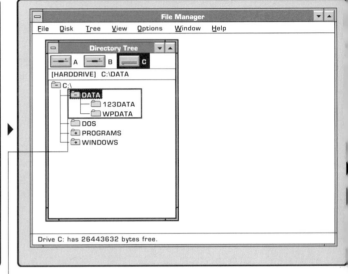

The (+) sign within a folder indicates that it contains one or more subdirectories.

■ Click the folder of the directory you want to expand (example: **DATA**).

■ The **DATA** folder is expanded to display its subdirectories **\123DATA** and **\WPDATA**.

Note: The (–) sign within a directory folder indicates that it is already expanded.

EXPAND AN ENTIRE BRANCH

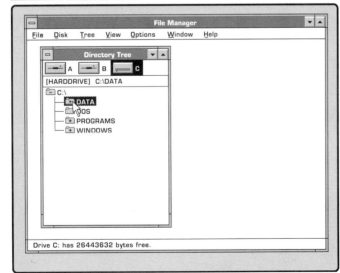 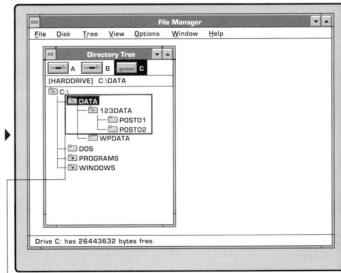

■ Press ↑ or ↓ to select the directory branch you would like to expand (example: **DATA**).

■ Press * (asterisk) and the entire branch of subdirectories under the **DATA** folder is displayed.

*Note: The subdirectories **\POST01** and **\POST02** were created the same way as the **\123DATA** and **\WPDATA** subdirectories on the previous page.*

EXPAND ALL BRANCHES

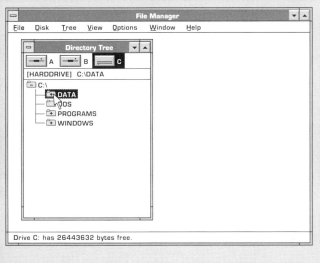

1 Press **Alt**,**T**,**A**.

■ All branches and all subdirectories are displayed.

COLLAPSE ALL DIRECTORY LEVELS

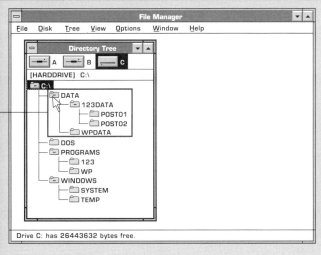

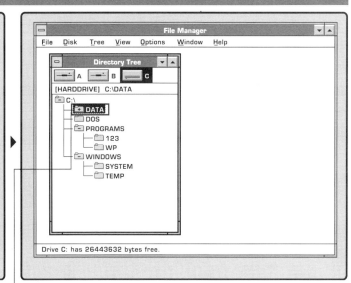

1 Click any folder containing a (–) sign (example: **DATA**).

■ The entire **DATA** branch collapses back into its folder.

Note: To collapse all directories and branches, click 📁 C:\ .

Windows Basics

Managing Your Programs

Managing Your Directories

Creating a File

Managing Your Files

Managing Your Diskettes

Help

MOVE OR COPY DIRECTORIES

MOVE A DIRECTORY WITHIN THE SAME DISK DRIVE

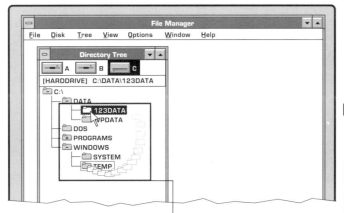 

Move a directory (example: \123DATA) into another directory (example: \TEMP) within the same disk drive. This is similar to moving a folder into another folder within the same filing cabinet.

1 Drag the **123DATA** folder over the **TEMP** folder. When a rectangle appears around 📁**TEMP**, release the mouse button. The dialog box on the next screen appears.

2 Click the **Yes** button or press **Enter** to continue.

or

Click the **No** button or press **Esc** to cancel the command.

COPY DIRECTORIES WITHIN THE SAME DISK DRIVE

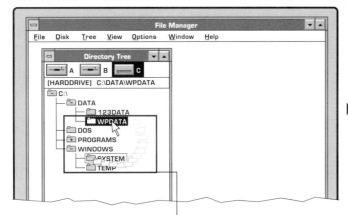 

Copy a directory (example: \WPDATA) into another directory (example: \SYS-TEM) within the same disk drive. This is similar to copying a folder and placing it into a different folder within the same filing cabinet.

1 Hold down **Ctrl** while you drag the **WPDATA** folder over the **SYSTEM** folder. Release the mouse button and then release **Ctrl**. The dialog box on the next screen appears.

2 Press **Enter** to continue.

or

Press **Esc** to cancel the command.

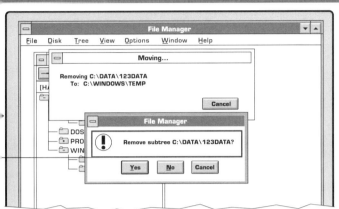

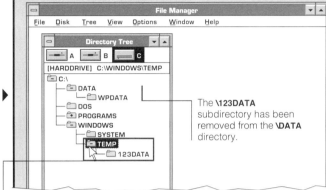

The **\123DATA** subdirectory has been removed from the **\DATA** directory.

■ Windows asks for your permission to remove the **\123DATA** subdirectory from the **\DATA** directory.

3 Press **Enter** and **\123DATA** directory is moved into the **TEMP** folder.

4 Click the **TEMP** folder to display its **\123DATA** subdirectory.

Note: If the **\123DATA** *subdirectory contained files, they would be moved at the same time.*

Note: On page 59 of this guide, you will be shown how to copy and move files and directories to other disk drives.

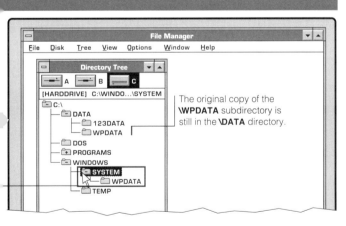

The original copy of the **\WPDATA** subdirectory is still in the **\DATA** directory.

3 Click the **SYSTEM** folder to display its **\WPDATA** subdirectory.

Note: If the **\WPDATA** *subdirectory contained files, they would have been copied at the same time.*

Windows Basics

Managing Your Programs

Managing Your Directories

Creating a File

Managing Your Files

Managing Your Diskettes

Help

DELETE DIRECTORIES

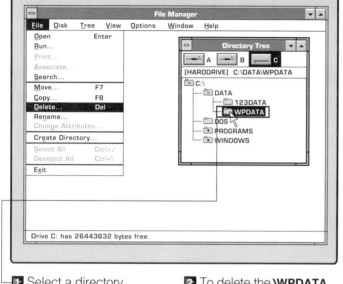

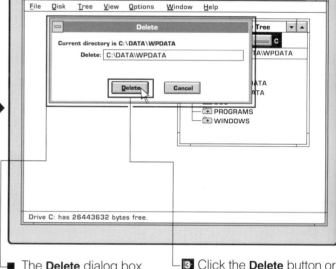

1 Select a directory (example: **WPDATA**) that you want to delete by clicking its folder.

2 To delete the **WPDATA** directory, press **Alt,F,D**.

☞ **Shortcut:**

Press **Del**.

■ The **Delete** dialog box appears.

3 Click the **Delete** button or press **Enter**.

or

Click the **Cancel** button or press **Esc** to cancel the command.

KEYBOARD SHORTCUTS TO SELECT COMMANDS

■ Some commands have keyboard shortcuts to select them. Keyboard shortcuts are listed to the right of the command (example: for Copy press **F8**, for Delete press **Del**).

Note: The shaded commands are not currently operational. For example, since no document is "selected", the Print command cannot be accessed.

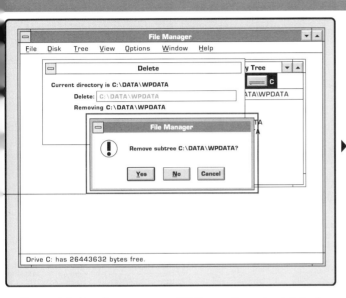

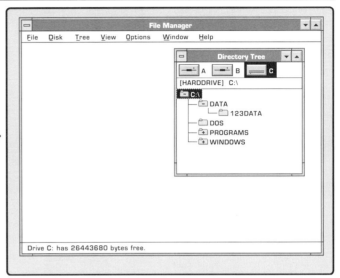

■ Since deleting the wrong directory could be a serious mistake, this confirmation request offers you a final chance to change your mind.

4 Press **Enter** to delete the **\WPDATA** directory.

or

Press **Esc** to cancel the command.

■ The **\WPDATA** directory is deleted.

Note: Windows will not delete a directory until all the files contained within it are erased.

When you try to delete a directory containing files, Windows asks you to confirm the deletion of each file, one at a time, before allowing you to delete the directory. This assumes that ⊠ Confirm on Delete is on.

CHECK OR CHANGE CONFIRMATION STATUS

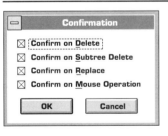

*Note: We recommend you keep all Confirmation options **on**.*

1 To check the Confirmation status, press **Alt**,**O**,**C**.

If all Confirmation options are **on**, each time you delete files and directories, replace files, or use the mouse to copy or move files—a Confirmation dialog box appears.

■ An empty box ☐ means a Confirmation option is **off**.

■ A box containing a cross ⊠ means a Confirmation option is **on**.

2 To toggle between **on** and **off**, click the box.

Windows Basics

Managing Your Programs

Managing Your Directories

Creating a File

Managing Your Files

Managing Your Diskettes

Help

◀ 37

START AN APPLICATION

1 Open the **Accessories** Group window by double clicking its icon.

2 Start an application (example: **Write**) by double clicking its icon.

Note: To keep the desktop uncluttered, you can minimize the existing application (example: Program Manager) when you start or open a new application (example: Write).

MINIMIZE AN APPLICATION ON US

Options
✓ **A**uto Arrange
✓ **M**inimize on Use

■ To check the status of **Minimize on Use**, press **Alt,O**.

■ If no checkmark is in front of **Minimize on Use**, it is *off*.

■ To turn it *on*, press **M**.

*Note: If a checkmark (✓) is already in front of **Minimize on Use**, it is **on** Press **Esc** to retain the setting.*

/ **Start an**
Application

Save
a File

Open
a File

Print
a File

Transfer Information
Between Applications

Exit an
Application

Most applications are used to create files. Typical files are letters, memos, worksheets, databases and graphic illustrations.

■3 Type the text displayed in the **Write** window.

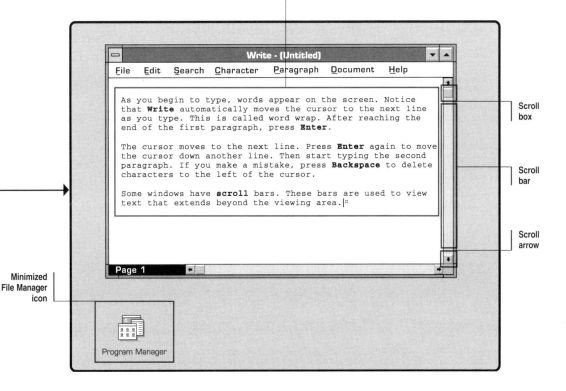

Scroll box

Scroll bar

Scroll arrow

Minimized File Manager icon

Program Manager

Windows Basics

Managing Your Programs

Managing Your Directories

Creating a File

Managing Your Files

Managing Your Diskettes

Help

SCROLLING DOCUMENTS

Scroll one line at a time	Click ⬆ or ⬇ . To continuously scroll line by line, click and hold down the left button.
Scroll one window up	Click in the scroll bar below the scroll box ▦ .
Scroll one window down	Click in the scroll bar above the scroll box ▦ .
Scroll to any position in the document	Drag the scroll box ▦ . To move proportionally (example: half way) down the document, drag the box proportionally (example: half way) down the scroll bar.
To move to the end of the document	Press **Ctrl+Home**
To move to the beginning of the document	Press **Ctrl+End**

SAVE A FILE

Save this document to drive C, \DATA\WPDATA directory and give it a name (example: test).

1 Click **File**. Its menu appears.

Note: A file is a document that you have named and saved to disk.

2 Click **Save**.

☞ **Shortcut:**

Press **Alt,F,S**.

■ A **File Save As** dialog box appears. The current directory is **c:\windows**.

■ **To change from the \WINDOWS directory to the \DATA\WPDATA directory you must follow the path shown:**

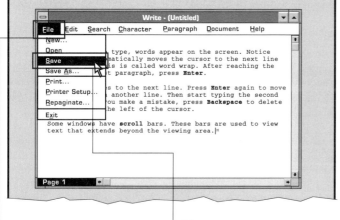

3 Double click **[..]** to change the current directory (c:\windows) to the **c:** or root directory.

■ The current directory is now **c:**.

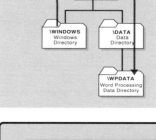

4 Double click **[data]** to change the current directory (c:\) to the **c:\data** directory.

Windows Basics

Managing Your Programs

Managing Your Directories

Creating a File

Managing Your Files

Managing Your Diskettes

Help

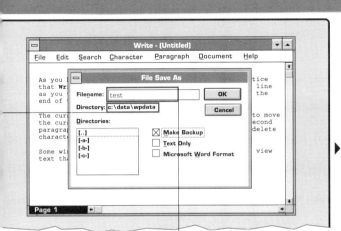

■ The current directory is now **c:\data\wpdata**.

6 Click in the **Filename** box and type a name (example: **test**). Then press **Enter** to save the file.

☞ Shortcut:

To replace steps **3** to **6**, type **\data\wpdata\test** and press **Enter**.

Note: Windows commands are not case sensitive. You can type \data\wpdata\test or \DATA\WPDATA\TEST.

7 To save future changes to the file saved in step **6**, press **Alt,F,S**.

or

To save the existing file and create a new file with a different name, press **Alt,F,A**. Type a new filename and select a directory to save the new file to.

Note: If an extension is not specified, many applications automatically add an extension (example: .WRI for Write or .BMP for Paintbrush) to the filename.

PRACTICE FILES

Normally, files are created using application software (such as word processing, spreadsheet, graphic packages, etc.). The method below is used to create practice files for the examples that follow in this guide.

1 To create a practice file from any Write document, press **Alt,F,A**.

2 Type the new **file specification** and press **Enter**.

Examples: (refer to page 25)

■ Type **C:\DATA\123DATA\INCOME1Q.WK1** and then press **Enter**. The file is copied to the drive C, \DATA\123DATA directory and named INCOME1Q.WK1.

■ Type **C:\DATA\WPDATA\MERGE.LET** and then press **Enter**. The file is copied to the drive C, \DATA\WPDATA directory and named MERGE.LET.

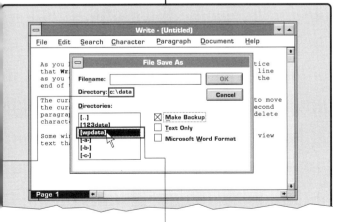

■ The current directory is now **c:\data**.

5 Double click **[wpdata]** to change the current directory (c:\data) to the **c:\data\wpdata** directory.

OPEN AN EXISTING FILE OR DOCUMENT

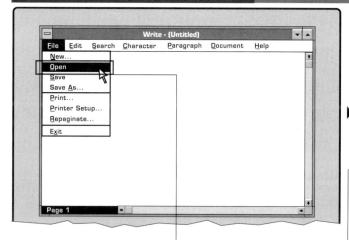

Let's assume you created a document in Write, named it training and saved it to drive c, \data\wpdata directory.

1 Start the **Write** application by double clicking its icon.

*Note: To open a file, you must start the application that created it (example: for a Notepad file start **Notepad**, for a Paintbrush file start **Paintbrush**).*

2 Click **File**. The File menu appears. Then click **Open**.

■ A **File Open** dialog box appears. The current directory is **c:\windows**.

■ The **Filename** box displays ⬛**.WRI**⬛. This means all files which end with the extension .WRI in the **c:\windows** directory are displayed in the **Files** box. None show so none exist.

3 Type *.* and press **Enter**.

USING THE *WILDCARD

When you use an * (asterisk) in a filename or extension, the * is interpreted to mean any number of characters, from one character up to an entire filename or extension. Typing *.* displays all the files in a directory.

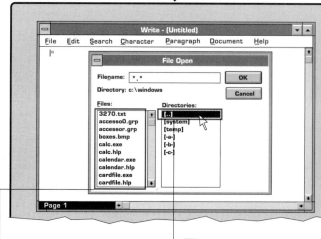

■ All these files exist in the **c:\windows** directory.

4 Double click **[..]** to change the current directory (c:\windows) to the **c:** or root directory.

Start an
Application

Save
a File

**Open
a File**

Print
a File

Transfer Information
Between Applications

Exit an
Application

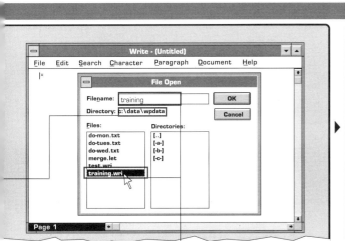

■ The current directory is now **c:\data\wpdata**.

7 Double click **training.wri**.

or

Drag over ***.*** to select it (the ***.*** becomes ▒). Type **training** and then press **Enter**.

☞ **Shortcut:**

To replace steps **3** to **7** , type **\data\wpdata\training** and press **Enter**.

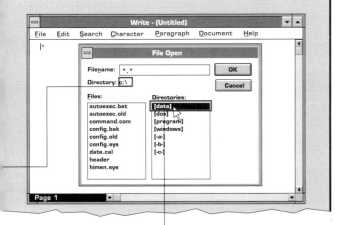

■ The current directory is now **c:**.

5 Double click **[data]** to change the current directory (c:\) to the **c:\data** directory.

6 Double click **[wpdata]** to change the current directory (c:\data) to the **c:\data\wpdata** directory.

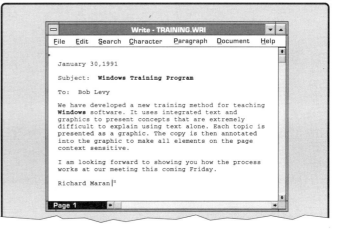

■ The **TRAINING.WRI** document is displayed.

*Note: If you do not specify an extension to a **WRITE** file, Windows automatically assigns the extension **.WRI** to it.*

TO OPEN A NEW FILE TO START ANOTHER LETTER

Press **Alt**,**F**,**N**.

**Windows
Basics**

**Managing
Your
Programs**

**Managing
Your
Directories**

**Creating
a File**

**Managing
Your
Files**

**Managing
Your
Diskettes**

Help

PRINT
A FILE

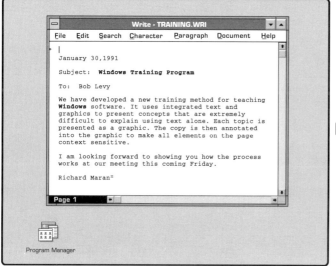

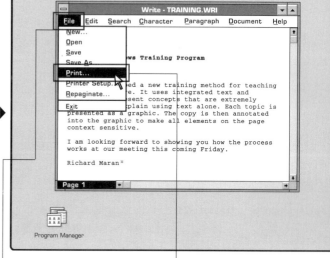

Before you can print a file or document, you must connect and install a printer.

For complete instructions on how to install a printer, refer to Microsoft Windows User's Guide.

1 Open the file you want to print (example: **TRAINING.WRI**).

Most applications designed to work with Windows have a Print command in their File menu. Each application offers its own formatting features and options to optimize the printed document.

Note: A document can be printed before it is saved.

2 Click **File**. The File menu appears.

3 Click **Print**.

☞ **Shortcut:**

Press **Alt,F,P**.

Start an
Application

Save
a File

Open
a File

**Print
a File**

Transfer Information
Between Applications

Exit an
Application

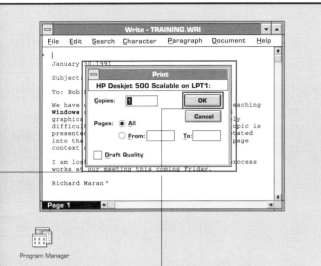

January 30,1991

Subject: **Windows Training Program**

To: Bob Levy

We have developed a new training method for teaching **Windows** software. It uses integrated text and graphics to present concepts that are extremely difficult to explain using text alone. Each topic is presented as a graphic. The copy is then annotated into the graphic to make all elements on the page context sensitive.

I am looking forward to showing you how the process works at our meeting this coming Friday.

Richard Maran

■ The **Print** dialog box appears.

Note: In this example, we are using a HP DeskJet 500 printer.

4 Select the options you require, and then click the **OK** button or press **Enter**.

■ Type in the number of copies you want to print. The default setting is **1**.

■ **All** is the default setting. All the pages in the document will be printed.

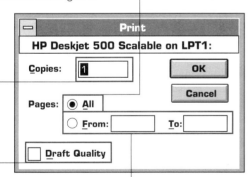

■ If you click the **Draft** box, the printer produces a fast, low quality image. Some printers do not support the Draft option.

■ Click in the **From** box and type the page number to start printing from. Then click in the **To** box and type the page number to print to.

Windows
Basics

Managing
Your
Programs

Managing
Your
Directories

Creating
a File

Managing
Your
Files

Managing
Your
Diskettes

Help

TRANSFER INFORMATION BETWEEN APPLICATIONS USING THE CLIPBOARD

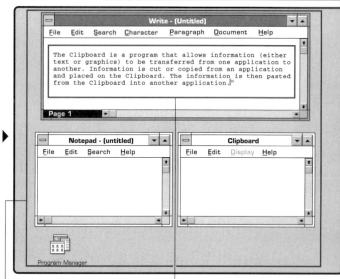

The Clipboard is a program that allows information to be transferred from one application to another.

Information is cut or copied from an application and placed on the Clipboard. The information is then pasted from the Clipboard into another application.

Information on the Clipboard can be pasted into the same or other applications as many times as is required. The Clipboard retains its information until you cut or copy new information to it, clear it or exit from Windows.

Note: Information can be either text or a combination of text and graphics. To transfer graphics, refer to your Microsoft Windows User's Guide.

For example, copy text from the Write application to the Notepad.

1 Start the **Write**, **Notepad** and **Clipboard** applications by double clicking their respective icons.

2 Minimize the **Program Manager** window and resize the other windows as shown above.

Note: To minimize and resize windows, refer to pages 6 to 9 of this guide.

3 Click in the **Write** window and then type the text shown above.

EXIT AN APPLICATION

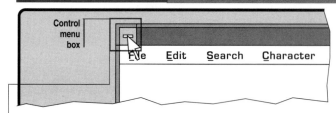

1 To exit any application, double click its **Control menu box**.

Note: If a change had been made to the document, since the last time it was saved, a dialog box appears asking you if you want to save the change before exiting the application.

Start an
Application

Save
a File

Open
a File

Print
a File

**Transfer Information
Between Applications**

**Exit an
Application**

Windows
Basics

Managing
Your
Programs

Managing
Your
Directories

Creating
a File

Managing
Your
Files

Managing
Your
Diskettes

Help

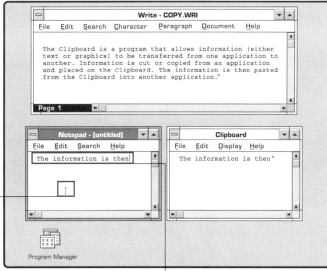

4 Select the text you want to copy to the Clipboard (example: **The information is then**). To select this text, move the mouse ☓ until it is to the left of the **T** in **The**. Click and drag the mouse over the text **The information is then**. As you drag, the letters turn white on a black background. Release the left button when you reach the end of the word **then**.

Note: For full details on selecting and editing text refer to the User's Manual for that specific application.

5 Press **Alt,E,C** to copy the selected text. The text is copied to the Clipboard.

☞ **Shortcut:**

Press **Ctrl+Ins**.

*Note: The **Copy** command copies information to the Clipboard, leaving the original information intact.*

*The **Cut** command removes the original information from the application and copies it to the Clipboard.*

6 Select the application (example: **Notepad**) that you want to paste the selected text into by clicking in its window.

Note: The Notepad is now the active application.

7 Press **Alt,E,P** to paste the selected text into the Notepad.

☞ **Shortcut:**

Press **Shift+Ins**.

Note: The Clipboard is open to help demonstrate how this process works. It does not have to be open to copy and paste the text between applications. Normally, the Clipboard is closed.

◄ 47

OPEN DIRECTORY WINDOWS

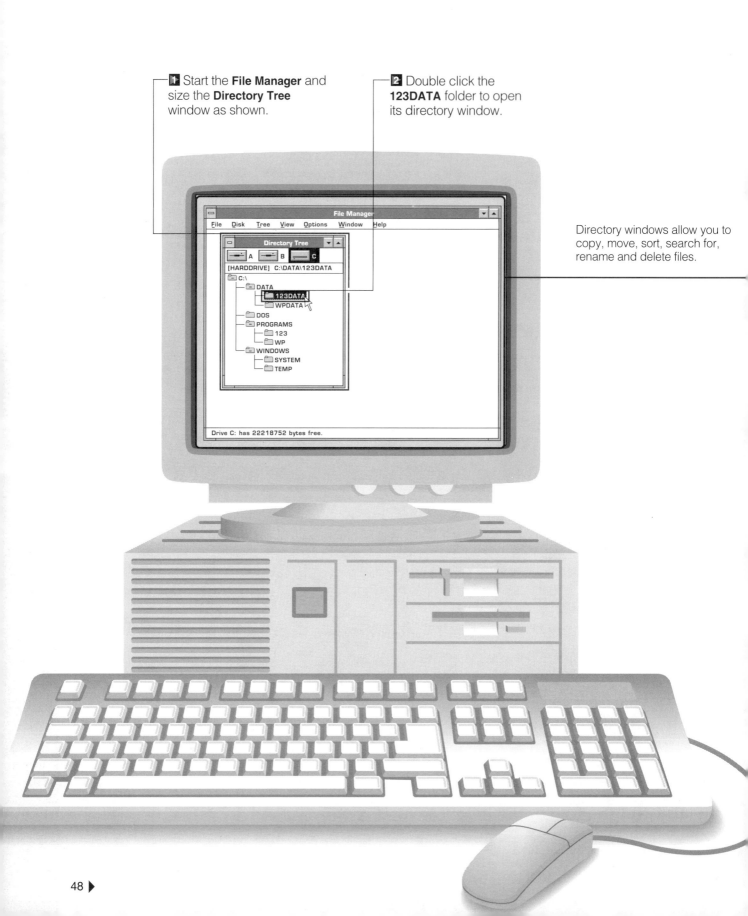

1 Start the **File Manager** and size the **Directory Tree** window as shown.

2 Double click the **123DATA** folder to open its directory window.

Directory windows allow you to copy, move, sort, search for, rename and delete files.

File Manager

File   Disk   Tree   View   Options   Window   Help

Directory Tree

A   B   C

[HARDDRIVE] C:\DATA\123DATA

C:\
  DATA
    123DATA
    WPDATA
  DOS
  PROGRAMS
    123
    WP
  WINDOWS
    SYSTEM
    TEMP

Drive C: has 22218752 bytes free.

The **Directory Tree** window allows you to open as many **directory** windows as required to manage your files.

Each **directory** window displays the files and subdirectories it contains.

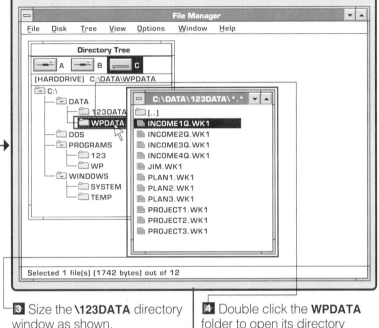

*Note: Only one **Directory Tree** window can be open at a time.*

3 Size the **\123DATA** directory window as shown.

4 Double click the **WPDATA** folder to open its directory window.

Note: To create practice files, refer to page 41.

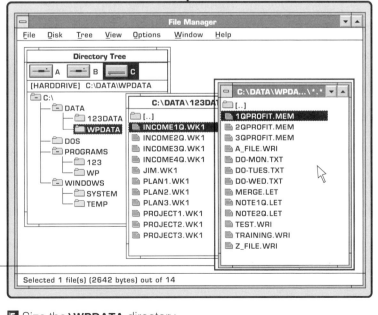

Note: To switch between directory windows, click anywhere in a window to select it.

*You can also switch between directory windows by pressing **Ctrl+Tab**.*

*Use the **Tile** command (press **Alt**,**W**,**T**) or the **Cascade** command (press **Alt**,**W**,**C**) to display all open directory windows.*

5 Size the **\WPDATA** directory window as shown.

Windows Basics

Managing Your Programs

Managing Your Directories

Creating a File

Managing Your Files

Managing Your Diskettes

Help

SEARCH FOR FILES USING THE * WILDCARD

When you use an * (asterisk) in a file name or extension within a Windows command, the * is interpreted to mean any number of characters, from one character up to an entire filename or extension. This is useful for finding files containing groups of characters (example: **BUDGET, NOTE, TRIP, WK1,** etc.).

Note: Files found in the Search Results window can be moved or copied to other directories. However, files from other directories cannot be moved or copied to the Search Results window.

Files in the Search Results window can also be deleted or renamed.

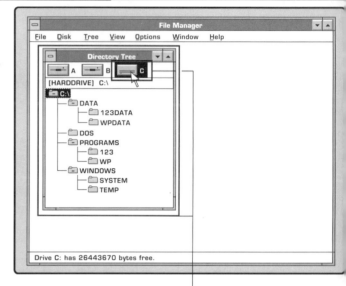

Search for all files on drive C with the extension .WK1.

1 Open the **File Manager**.

2 Resize the **Directory Tree** window as shown and then click drive icon **C** to select it.

SEARCH FOR FILES USING THE ? WILDCARD

When you use a ? (question mark) in a filename or extension, the ? is interpreted to mean any character in that position. This is useful for finding files with similar names.

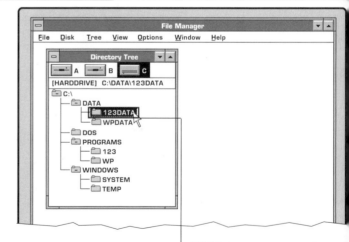

Search for all files on drive C, \DATA\123DATA directory whose filenames begin with INCOME and end with Q, with the extension .WK1.

1 Click the **123DATA** folder to select its directory.

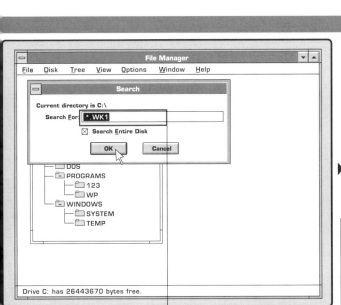

3 Press **Alt**,**F**,**H** and the **Search** window appears.

4 Type ***.WK1** and then click the **OK** button.

Note: To search for a specific file (example: PLAN1.WK1), type PLAN1.WK1 and press Enter.

■ The search found **11** files in the **C:\DATA\123DATA** directory and **2** files in the **C:\PROGRAMS\123** directory that satisfied the search criteria.

Windows Basics

Managing Your Programs

Managing Your Directories

Creating a File

Managing Your Files

Managing Your Diskettes

Help

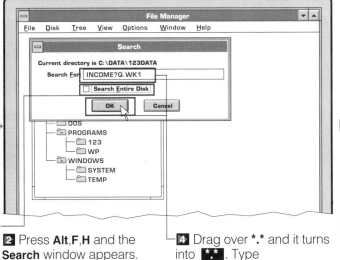

2 Press **Alt**,**F**,**H** and the **Search** window appears.

3 Click the **Search Entire Disk** box to turn it *off*.

Note: This speeds up the search process because only the C:\DATA\123DATA directory is searched.

4 Drag over ***.*** and it turns into **▨**. Type **INCOME?Q.WK1** and then click the **OK** button.

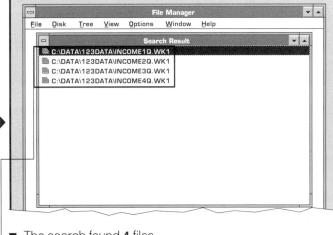

■ The search found **4** files in the **C:\DATA\123DATA** directory that satisfied the search criteria.

SELECT MULTIPLE FILES

SELECT A GROUP OF FILES IN SEQUENCE

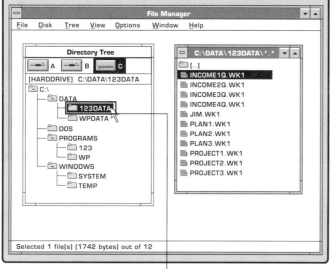

Multiple file selection is very useful for moving, copying and deleting groups of files or directories.

1 Double click the **123DATA** folder to open the \123DATA directory window.

2 Click a file to start the group (example: **PROJECT1.WK1**).

3 To select the group, hold down **Shift** and click the file at the end of the group (example: **PROJECT3.WK1**).

SELECT TWO OR MORE FILES RANDOMLY

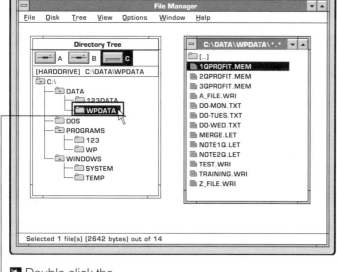

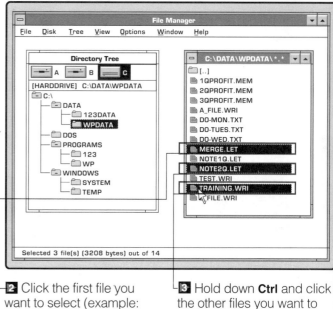

1 Double click the **WPDATA** folder to open the \WPDATA directory window.

2 Click the first file you want to select (example: **MERGE.LET**).

3 Hold down **Ctrl** and click the other files you want to select (example: **NOTE2Q.LET** and **TRAINING.WRI**).

SELECT MULTIPLE GROUPS OF FILES

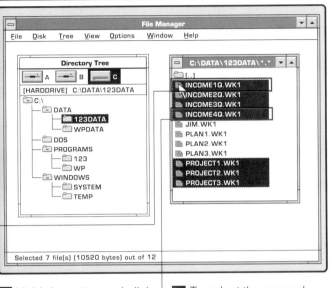

Note: To cancel any group of sequential or randomly selected files, click on any file in the window.

4 Hold down **Ctrl** and click the first file of the second group (example: **INCOME1Q.WK1**).

5 To select the second group, hold down **Ctrl+Shift** and click the file at the end of the second group (example: **INCOME4Q.WK1**).

SELECT ALL FILES

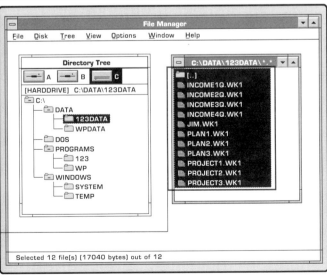

1 To select all files, press **Ctrl+/** (slash).

DESELECT ALL FILES

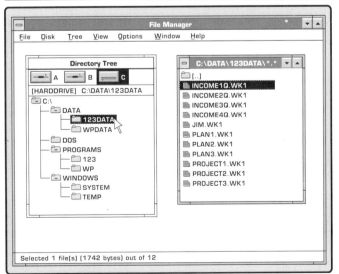

1 To deselect all files, press **Ctrl+** (backslash).

*Note: To deselect a single file, hold down **Ctrl** and click that file.*

Windows Basics

Managing Your Programs

Managing Your Directories

Creating a File

Managing Your Files

Managing Your Diskettes

Help

DISPLAY FILE INFORMATION

CHANGE FILE INFORMATION DISPLAY

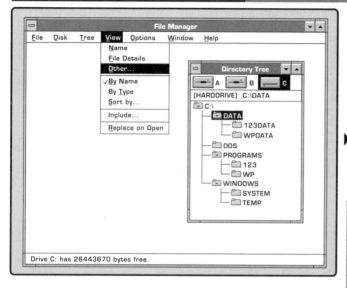

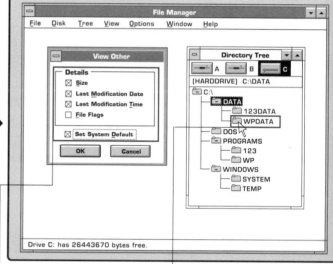

You can change the way file information is displayed in a directory window.

1 Press **Alt,V,O** to select the **View Other** dialog box.

*Note: If the **Directory Tree** window is active when you make changes to the **View Other** dialog box, all directory windows opened afterwards incorporate those changes.*

2 The **View Other** dialog box allows you to change the file information displayed in a directory window. Click the **File Flags** box to turn if *off*.

3 Click **OK** or press **Enter**.

4 Click the **WPDATA** folder to open its directory window.

DIALOG BOX EXPLANATIONS

☒ Size

Includes the size (in bytes) of each file.

☒ Last Modification Date

Includes the date the file was last modified.

☒ Last Modification Time

Includes the time the file was last modified.

☐ File Flags

This is for advanced users. Refer to your Microsoft Windows User's Guide.

SET SYSTEM DEFAULT

If a directory window is active when you access the **View Others** dialog box, changes made only apply to that directory window.

If you want the changes to apply to all subsequent directory windows that are opened, click the **Set System Default** box to turn it *on*.

*Note: ☒ means it's **on**,*
*☐ means it's **off**.*

*To toggle between **on** and **off**, click the box.*

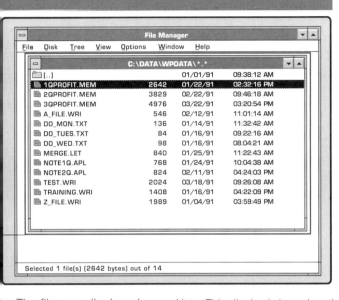

■ The files are displayed including Size, Last Modification Date and Last Modification Time.

Note: This display is based on the settings chosen in step **2** *.*

DISPLAY FILES

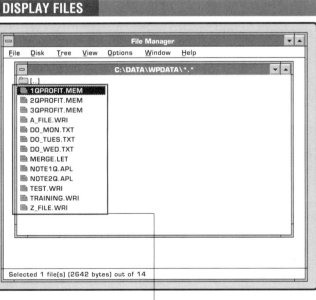

1 Press **Alt,V,N**.

*Note: This command overrides the **View Other** dialog box settings.*

■ Filenames are displayed numerically and alphabetically in descending order.

DISPLAY FILE DETAILS

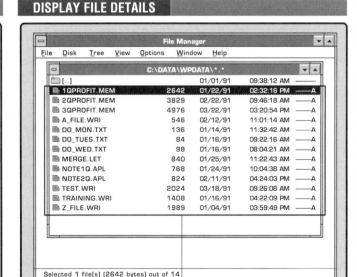

1 Press **Alt,V,F**.

*Note: This command overrides the **View Other** dialog box settings.*

■ Complete file information is displayed including Size, Last Modification Date/Time and File Flags status.

Windows Basics

Managing Your Programs

Managing Your Directories

Creating a File

Managing Your Files

Managing Your Diskettes

Help

SORT FILES

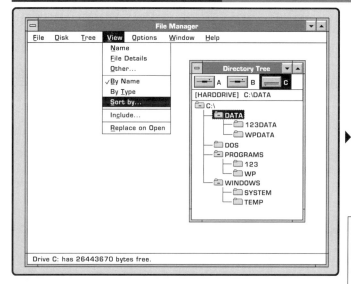

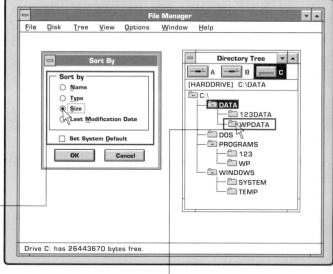

Files can be sorted alphabetically by Filename Extension, Size or Last Modification Date.

*Note: This assumes the **View Other** dialog box has been set as per step **2** on page 54.*

Files organized and sorted these ways permit efficient evaluation and management of your data (example: for possible deletion of old files, analysis of large files and alphabetic grouping and review of files with common extensions).

1 Press **Alt,V,S** to select the **Sort By** dialog box.

*Note: If the Directory Tree window is active when you make changes to **Sort By** dialog box, all directory windows opened afterwards incorporate those changes.*

2 The **Sort By** dialog box allows you to choose the way the files are sorted. Click **Size** for the screen example that follows.

3 Click **OK** or press **Enter**.

4 Double click the **WPDATA** folder to open its directory window.

CLICK ON

○ **Name**
To sort by filename in alphabetical order.

or

○ **Type**
To sort by file extension in alphabetical order.

or

○ **Size**
To sort by file size starting with the largest file.

or

○ **Last Modification Date**
To sort by last modification date, displaying the most recently modified files first.

SET SYSTEM DEFAULTS

If a directory window is active when you access the **Sort By** dialog box, changes made only apply to that directory window.

If you want the changes to apply to all subsequent directory windows that are opened, click the **Set System Default** box to turn it *on*.

*Note: ● means it's **on**,*
*○ means it's **off**.*

*To toggle between **on** and **off**, click the box.*

SORT BY SIZE

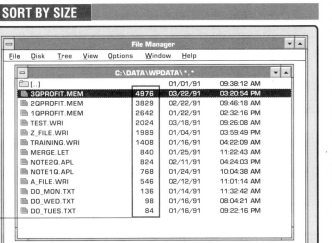

■ The files are sorted by file size, starting with the largest.

SORT BY FILENAME

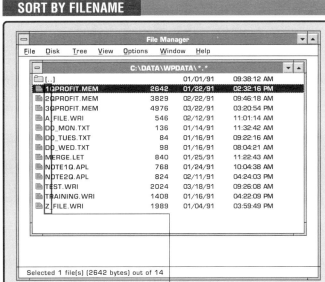

1 Press **Alt,V,B**.

*Note: This command overrides the **Sort By** dialog box.*

■ The files are sorted by filename in alphabetical order.

SORT BY LAST MODIFICATION DATE

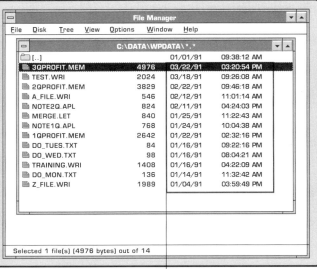

1 Click **Last Modification Date** in step **2**. Then proceed with steps **3** and **4**.

■ The files are sorted by Last Modification Date, displaying the most recently modified files first.

SORT BY FILE TYPE

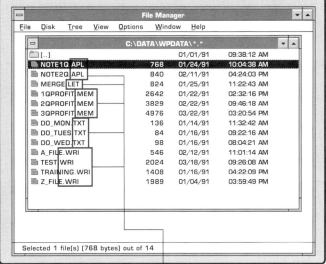

1 Press **Alt,V,T**.

*Note: This command overrides the **Sort By** dialog box.*

■ The files are sorted by file type or extension in alphabetical order.

Windows Basics

Managing Your Programs

Managing Your Directories

Creating a File

Managing Your Files

Managing Your Diskettes

Help

COPY OR MOVE FILES

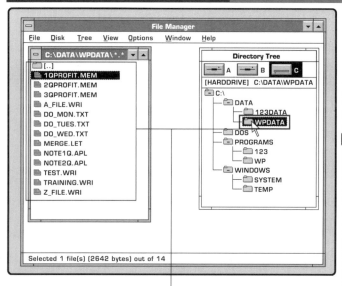

Suppose you want to copy files DO_MON.TXT, DO_TUES.TXT, and DO_WED.TXT in drive C, \DATA\WPDATA directory to the root directory of a diskette in drive A.

This is useful for backing up selected data files to a diskette.

Note: You can use this same procedure in reverse to copy files from a diskette in drive A to any directory in drive C.

1 Double click the **WPDATA** folder to display the files in its directory window.

2 Click drive icon **A** to make it the current drive.

3 Select files **DO_MON.TXT DO_TUES.TXT** and **DO_WED.TXT** and drag them over the **A:** folder. When the files 📁 are over the **A:** folder, a rectangle appears around it. Then release the mouse button.

Note: Refer to page 52 for selecting multiple files.

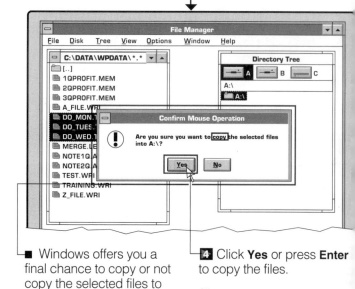

■ Windows offers you a final chance to copy or not copy the selected files to the diskette in drive A.

4 Click **Yes** or press **Enter** to copy the files.

or

Click the **No** button to cancel the command.

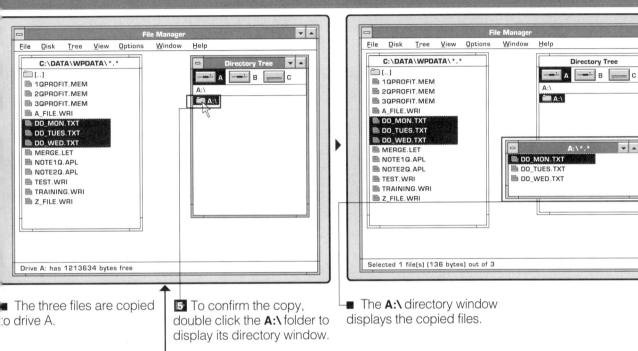

■ The three files are copied to drive A.

5 To confirm the copy, double click the **A:** folder to display its directory window.

■ The **A:** directory window displays the copied files.

Windows
Basics

Managing
Your
Programs

Managing
Your
Directories

Creating
a File

**Managing
Your
Files**

Managing
Your
Diskettes

Help

TO MOVE FILES INSTEAD OF COPYING THEM

The same procedure applies, except hold down **Alt** before you drag the files over folder **A:** in step **3** . Release the mouse button and then release **Alt**.

*Note: The **Confirm Mouse Operation** dialog box in step* **4** *displays "Are you sure you want to **move** the selected files into A:\?".*

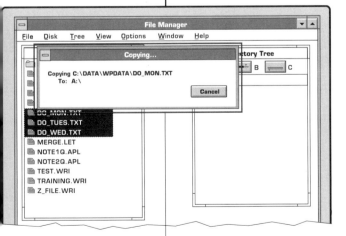

■ A dialog box appears indicating copying is in progress.

Note: Confirmation dialog boxes can be suppressed. Refer to page 37.

COPY OR MOVE FILES

COPY DIRECTORIES CONTAINING FILES TO A DIFFERENT DRIVE

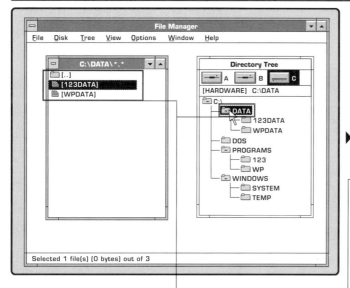

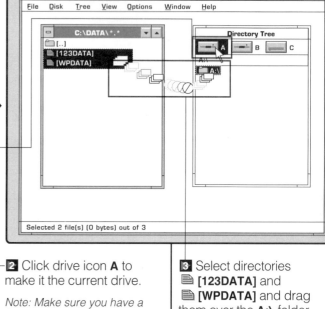

Suppose you want to copy data directories 📄 **[123DATA] and** 📄 **[WPDATA] containing all your data files to a diskette in drive A.**

This is useful for backing up all your data files at the same time.

Note: You can use this same procedure in reverse to copy directories from the diskette in drive A to any directory in drive C.

1 Double click the **DATA** folder to display the directory window containing 📄 **[123DATA]** and 📄 **[WPDATA]**.

2 Click drive icon **A** to make it the current drive.

Note: Make sure you have a formatted diskette in drive A.

3 Select directories 📄 **[123DATA]** and 📄 **[WPDATA]** and drag them over the **A:** folder. When the files 📄 are over the **A:** folder, a rectangle appears around it. Then release the mouse button.

Note: Refer to page 52 for selecting multiple files.

■ Windows offers you a final chance to copy or not copy the selected directories and their files to drive A.

4 Click the **Yes** button or press **Enter** to copy the directories.

Open Directory
Windows

Search for
Files

Select Multiple
Files

Display File
Information

Sort
Files

**Copy or
Move Files**

Rename
Files

Delete
Files

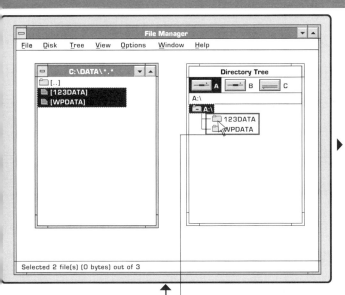

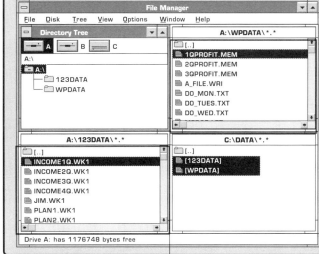

■ The two directories and all their files are copied to drive A.

5 To confirm the copy, double click folder **123DATA** and then double click folder **WPDATA** to display their directories.

6 Press **Alt,W,T** to **Tile** all the open windows.

└─ ■ The copied directories and their files are displayed.

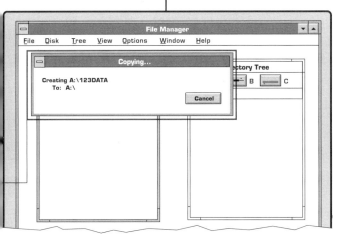

■ A dialog box appears indicating copying is in progress.

Note: To suppress Confirmation Dialog boxes, refer to page 37.

TO MOVE THE DIRECTORIES INSTEAD OF COPYING THEM

The same procedure applies, except hold down **Alt** before you drag the directories over folder **A:** in step **3**. Release the mouse button and then release **Alt**.

Note: The **Confirm Mouse Operation** dialog box in step **4** displays "Are you sure you want to **move** the selected files into A:\?".

Windows
Basics

Managing
Your
Programs

Managing
Your
Directories

Creating
a File

Managing
Your
Files

Managing
Your
Diskettes

Help

COPY OR MOVE FILES

COPY A FILE WITHIN THE SAME DIRECTORY

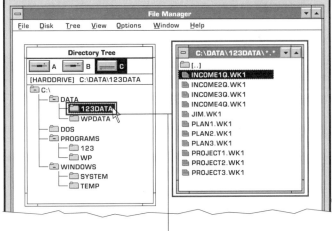

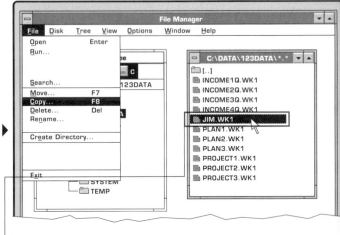

Copy JIM.WK1 within the same directory and name the copy JIMCOPY.WK1.

1 Double click the **123DATA** folder to open its directory window.

2 Click **JIM.WK1** to select it.

3 Press **Alt,F,C** to copy the file.

☞ **Shortcut:**

Press **F8**.

COPY FILES FROM ONE DIRECTORY TO ANOTHER WITHIN THE SAME DRIVE

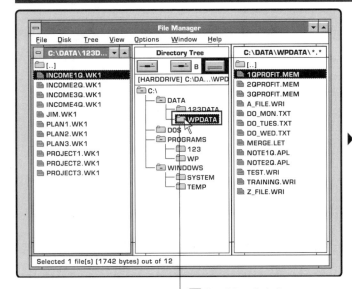

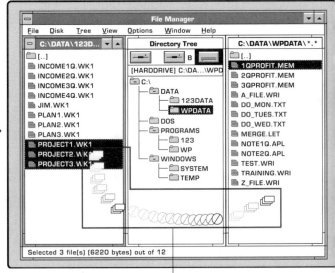

Copy PROJECT1.WK1, PROJECT2.WK1 and PROJECT3.WK1 within the same drive from the \123DATA directory to the \WPDATA directory.

1 Double click the **123DATA** and **WPDATA** folders to display their directory windows. Then press **Alt,W,T** to Tile the windows.

2 Select **PROJECT1.WK1**, **PROJECT2.WK1** and **PROJECT3.WK1**.

Note: To select multiple files refer to page 52.

3 Hold down **Ctrl** and drag the 3 files into the **\WPDATA** directory window. Release the mouse button and then release **Ctrl**.

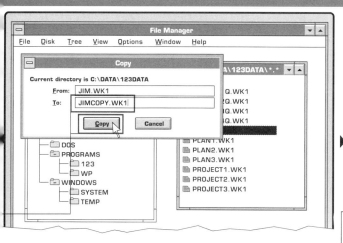

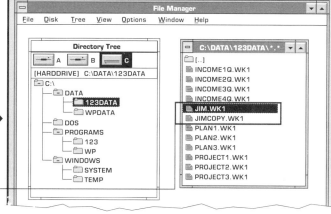

4 Type **JIMCOPY.WK1** and then click the **Copy** button or press **Enter**.

Note: When you copy a file within the same directory, its name must be changed. Each file in a directory must have a unique name.

■ The original file **JIM.WK1** and the copied file **JIMCOPY.WK1** now reside within the same directory window.

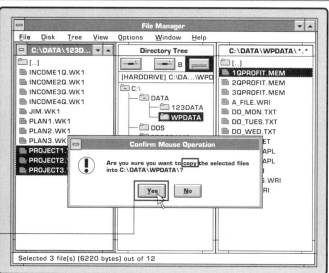

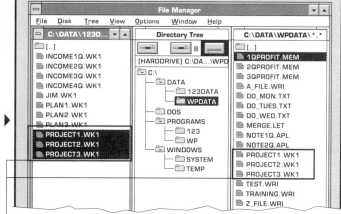

4 Click the **Yes** button or press **Enter** to copy the selected files.

or

Click the **No** button or press **Esc** to cancel the command.

■ The files **PROJECT1.WK1**, **PROJECT2.WK1** and **PROJECT3.WK1** are copied and now reside in both directory windows.

TO MOVE FILES FROM ONE DIRECTORY TO ANOTHER

Start at step **3**, but do not hold down **Ctrl**.

*Note: The **Confirm Mouse Operation** dialog box in step **4** then displays "Are you sure you want to **move** the selected files into C:\DATA\WPDATA?".*

Windows Basics

Managing Your Programs

Managing Your Directories

Creating a File

Managing Your Files

Managing Your Diskettes

Help

COPY OR
MOVE FILES

CREATE A NEW GROUP WINDOW

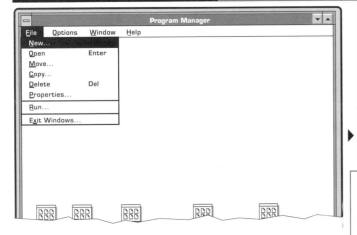

Suppose you are working on a project that uses several programs and data files. A new Group window can be created to hold and manage these files in one central location.

1 Press **Alt,F,N** to access the **New Program Object** dialog box. It appears on the next screen.

2 Click **Program Group** to select it. Then click the **OK** button or press **Enter**.

COPY FILES TO A GROUP WINDOW

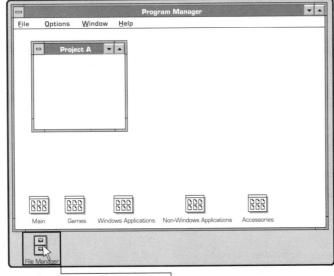

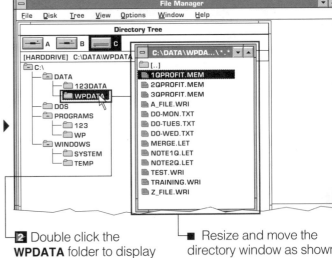

2 Double click the **WPDATA** folder to display its directory window.

■ Resize and move the directory window as shown above.

Files can be copied from any directory into a Group window. These files can then be started from the Group window.

Copy a file (example: TRAINING.WRI in the \WPDATA directory window) to the Project A Group window.

1 Double click the **File Manager** to start it.

Windows
Basics

Managing
Your
Programs

Managing
Your
Directories

Creating
a File

Managing
Your
Files

Managing
Your
Diskettes

Help

◄ **The Program Group Properties** dialog box appears.

3 Type the name of the new Group window (example: **Project A**) and then click the **OK** button or press **Enter**.

4 The new Group window entitled **Project A** appears. Resize the window as shown.

COPY OR MOVE A PROGRAM ITEM ICON

To **copy** a Program item icon from one Group window to another, hold down **Ctrl** and drag the icon between the windows. Release the mouse button and then **Ctrl**.

To **move** a Program item icon from one Group window to another, drag the item between the windows.

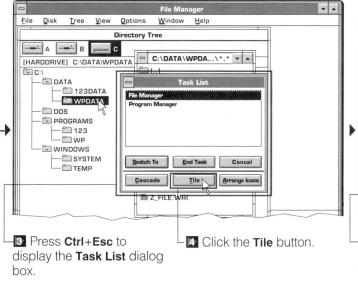

3 Press **Ctrl+Esc** to display the **Task List** dialog box.

4 Click the **Tile** button.

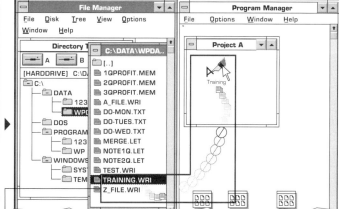

5 Click on the file you want to copy (example: **TRAINING.WRI**) and drag it into the **Project A** Group window. When you release the button, the **Training** file is copied and appears as a Program Item icon named **Training**.

DELETE A PROGRAM ITEM ICON

Click the icon to select it (example: **Training**). Then press **Del** and click the **Yes** button.

RENAME FILES

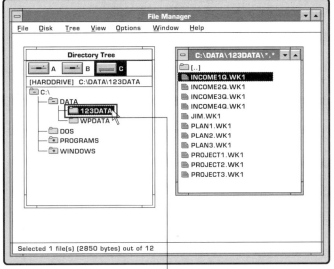

Rename the file INCOME3Q.WK1 to BUDGET3Q.WK1 in the \123DATA directory window.

1 Double click the **123DATA** folder to open the **\123DATA** directory window. Resize the window as shown above.

2 Click the file **INCOME3Q.WK1** to select it.

3 Press **Alt,F,N** to access the **Rename** dialog box.

Open Directory
Windows

Search for
Files

Select Multiple
Files

Display File
Information

Sort
Files

Copy or
Move Files

**Rename
Files**

Delete
Files

Windows
Basics

Managing
Your
Programs

Managing
Your
Directories

Creating
a File

Managing
Your
Files

Managing
Your
Diskettes

Help

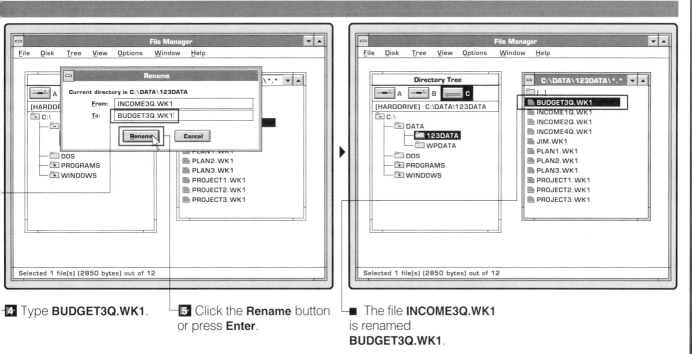

◀ Type **BUDGET3Q.WK1**.

▐5▌ Click the **Rename** button or press **Enter**.

■ The file **INCOME3Q.WK1** is renamed **BUDGET3Q.WK1**.

DELETE FILES

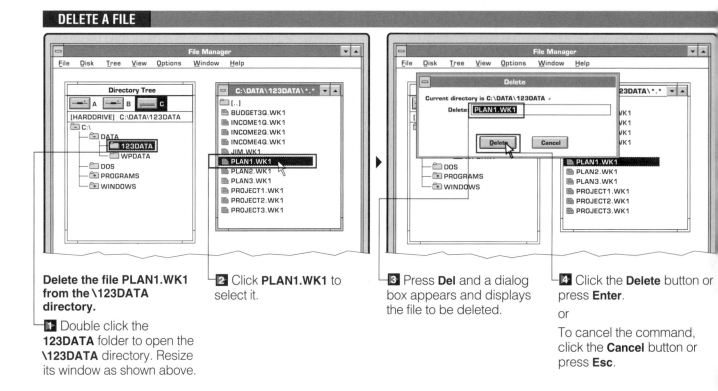

Delete the file PLAN1.WK1 from the \123DATA directory.

1 Double click the **123DATA** folder to open the **\123DATA** directory. Resize its window as shown above.

2 Click **PLAN1.WK1** to select it.

3 Press **Del** and a dialog box appears and displays the file to be deleted.

4 Click the **Delete** button or press **Enter**.

or

To cancel the command, click the **Cancel** button or press **Esc**.

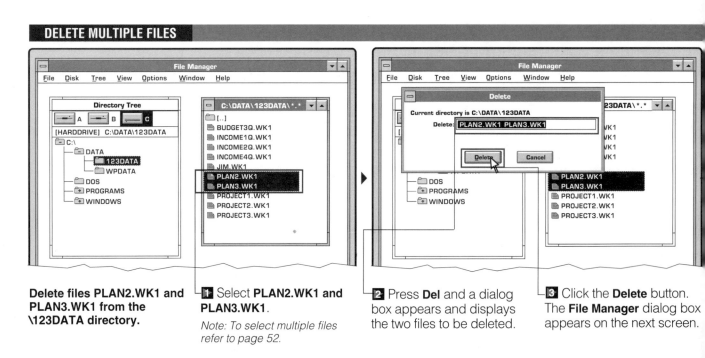

Delete files PLAN2.WK1 and PLAN3.WK1 from the \123DATA directory.

1 Select **PLAN2.WK1** and **PLAN3.WK1**.

Note: To select multiple files refer to page 52.

2 Press **Del** and a dialog box appears and displays the two files to be deleted.

3 Click the **Delete** button. The **File Manager** dialog box appears on the next screen.

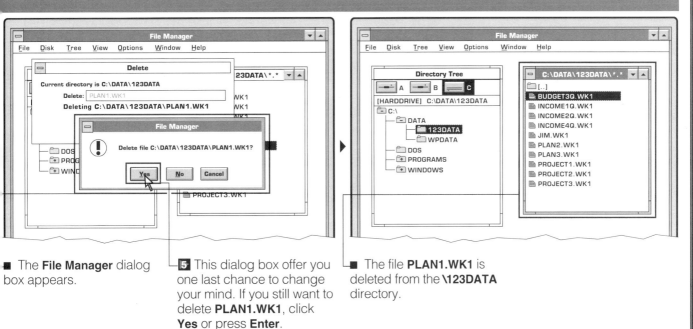

■ The **File Manager** dialog box appears.

5 This dialog box offer you one last chance to change your mind. If you still want to delete **PLAN1.WK1**, click **Yes** or press **Enter**.

■ The file **PLAN1.WK1** is deleted from the **\123DATA** directory.

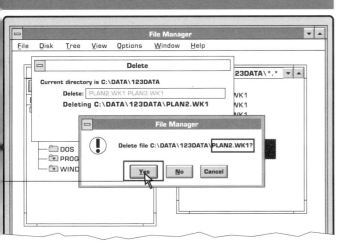

4 Click the **Yes** button to delete **PLAN2.WK1**.

or

Click the **No** button if you do not want to delete this file.

or

Click the **Cancel** button to cancel the Delete command.

5 If you clicked **Yes** or **No** in step **4**, another dialog box appears asking if you want to delete **PLAN3.WK1**. Click **Yes**.

Note: If more files were selected, this process continues until all selected files are deleted.

CHECK OR CHANGE CONFIRMATION STATUS

Note: We recommend you keep all Confirmation options on.

1 To check the Confirmation status, press **Alt,O,C**.

If all Confirmation options are **on**, each time you delete files and directories, replace files, or use the mouse to copy or move files—a Confirmation dialog box appears.

■ An empty box □ means a Confirmation option is **off**.

■ A box containing a cross ⊠ means a Confirmation option is **on**.

2 To toggle between **on** and **off**, click the box.

Windows Basics

Managing Your Programs

Managing Your Directories

Creating a File

Managing Your Files

Managing Your Diskettes

Help

FORMAT A DISKETTE

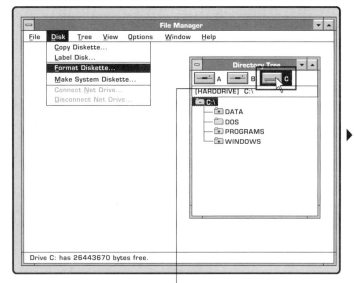

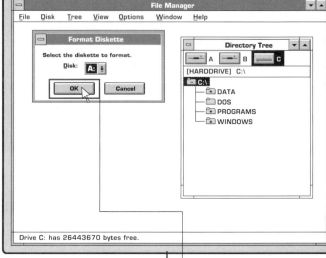

The Format Diskette command prepares a new or previously formatted diskette for storage of data program files.

1 Insert the diskette to be formatted into drive **A**.

2 Start the **File Manager** and click the drive **C** icon to make it the current drive.

3 To format the diskette in drive **A**, press **Alt,D,F**.

■ The **Format Diskette** dialog box only appears if your computer has two diskette drives (A and B).

Note: To format diskette B click ⬇ *. A menu appears. Click **B** to select its drive.*

4 Click the **OK** button or press **Enter**.

or

Click the **Cancel** button or press **Esc** to cancel the command.

Caution

The Format Diskette command destroys all information on the diskette being formatted. Do not format a diskette containing information you want to retain.

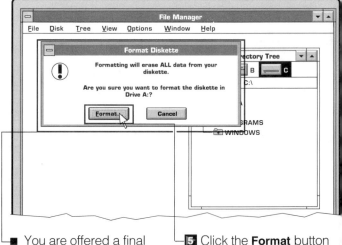

■ You are offered a final chance to change your mind.

5 Click the **Format** button to proceed.

or

Click the **Cancel** button to cancel the command.

Windows
Basics

Managing
Your
Programs

Managing
Your
Directories

Creating
a File

Managing
Your
Files

Managing
Your
Diskettes

Help

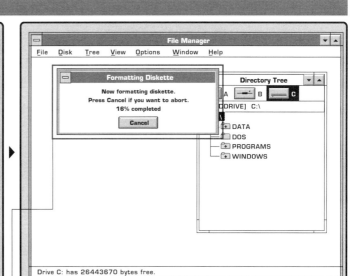

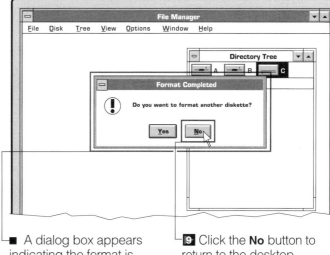

6 Select the capacity for the diskette you are about to format. Click the box to toggle between high and standard capacity.

If the box contains a ⊠, the diskette is formatted high capacity.

If the box is empty □, the diskette is formatted standard capacity.

Size	**Capacity**	
	High	**Standard**
5.25 inch	1.2 MB	360 K
3.5 inch	1.44 MB	720 K

Note: K is an abbreviation for Kilobytes (1,024 bytes). A byte represents one character.

MB is an abbreviation for Megabytes (1,048,576 bytes).

7 To include the system startup files, click the **Make System Disk** box □ to make it include an ⊠.

You can then start DOS directly from the diskette.

8 Press **Enter** to start formatting the diskette.

■ A dialog box appears displaying the progress of the formatting process.

■ A dialog box appears indicating the format is complete.

9 Click the **No** button to return to the desktop.

or

Click the **Yes** button to format another diskette.

COPY A DISKETTE

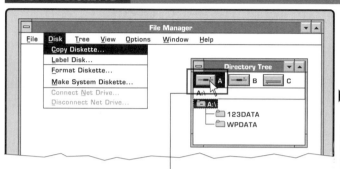

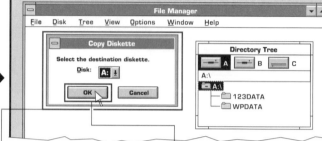

The Copy Diskette command is used to copy the entire contents of one diskette (the source) to another diskette (the destination), so that the second diskette is an exact copy of the first. This command only works on diskettes of the same size and capacity.

1 Insert a diskette into drive **A**.

2 Click the drive **A** icon to select it.

3 Press **Alt,D,C** to start the Copy Diskette process.

Note: To copy files between diskettes of different capacities, use the Copy command on pages 58 and 59.

■ The **Copy Diskette** dialog box only appears if your computer has two diskette drives (A and B).

Note: For computers with one diskette drive, the destination diskette does not have to be specified.

4 Click the **OK** button or press **Enter**.

or

Click the **Cancel** button or press **Esc** to cancel the command.

Caution

The Copy Diskette command automatically formats the destination diskette during the copy process. Make sure the destination diskette does not contain any files that you want to keep.

LABEL A DISKETTE OR DISK

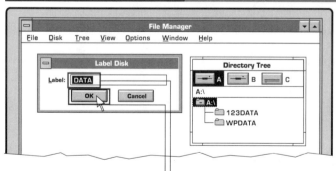

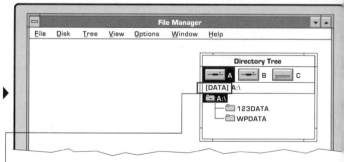

You can add a label to a diskette or change the existing label. Labels are useful to describe the contents of a diskette or disk.

1 Click the drive containing the disk (example: drive **A**) you want to label.

2 Press **Alt,D,L** to access the **Label Disk** dialog box.

3 Add a label (example: DATA) by typing **DATA**.

Note: To change a label, type the new label name. It will replace the existing label.

4 Click the **OK** button.

■ The new label **DATA** appears in the Directory Tree window.

Note: You can also add a label or change an existing label on your hard disk using the same command.

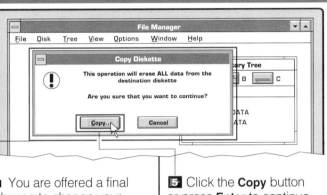

■ You are offered a final chance to change your mind.

5 Click the **Copy** button or press **Enter** to continue.

■ A dialog box appears showing the **destination** diskette receiving the copy.

■ The dialog box disappears after the **destination** diskette receives the copy.

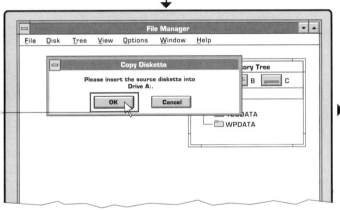

6 If the diskette currently in drive **A** is one you want to copy from, press the **OK** button or press **Enter**. This diskette is called the source diskette.

Note: If you want to copy some other diskette, you can exchange them at this point.

■ A dialog box appears showing the **source** diskette being copied.

7 The **Copy Diskette** dialog box appears at the completion of the **source** diskette copying.

Remove the **source** diskette and insert the **destination** diskette. Then click the **OK** button.

Note: The diskettes may have to be exchanged several times, depending on the amount of data copied.

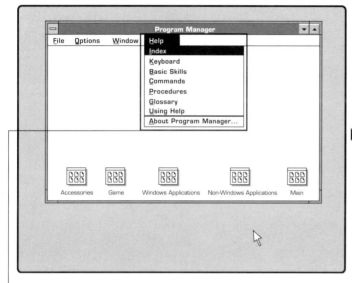

On-line Help provides information on basic skills, commands and procedures.

1 Press **Alt**,**H** to display the Help menu. Since the current or active application is the Program Manager, its Help menu is displayed.

Note: Each program in Windows (Write, Notepad, Paintbrush, etc.) has its own on-line Help. Windows programs supplied by other vendors usually have on-line Help that works in a similar way.

2 Select the topic of interest by pressing its underlined letter (example: **I** for **I**ndex).

☞ Shortcut:

Press **F1** to open the **Help Index** for the current or active application.

■ The **Program Manager Help** window appears.

3 Click the **Maximize** button to enlarge the **Program Manager Help** window.

ADDITIONAL NAVIGATION CHOICES

Click this button to view the Help Index for the active program.

Click this button to retrace your path back to the Help Index.

Click this button to move backward through a series of related topics.

Click this button to move forward through a series of related topics.

Note: When a button dims you have reached the first or last topic in the series.

Click this button to search for information on a specific word or phrase.

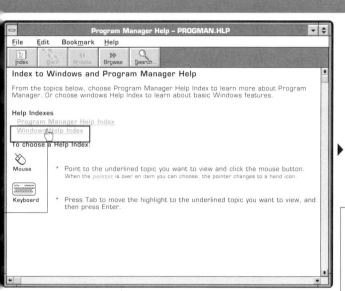

Program Manager Help – PROGMAN.HLP

File   Edit   Bookmark   Help

Index   Back   Browse   Browse   Search...

Index to Windows and Program Manager Help

From the topics below, choose Program Manager Help Index to learn more about Program Manager. Or choose windows Help Index to learn about basic Windows features.

Help Indexes
Program Manager Help Index
Windows Help Index

To choose a Help Index:

Mouse   *   Point to the underlined topic you want to view and click the mouse button. When the *pointer* is over an item you can choose, the pointer changes to a hand icon.

Keyboard   *   Press Tab to move the highlight to the underlined topic you want to view, and then press Enter.

Program Manager Help – PROGMAN.HLP

Edit   Bookmark   Help

Index   Back   Browse   Browse   Search...

Windows Help Index

The Index lists Help topics for learning about Windows. Index items are arranged alphabetically within each category. Use the scroll bar to see entries not currently visible in the Help window.

To learn how to use Help, press F1 or choose Using Help from the Help menu.

Keyboard
Cursor Movement Keys
Dialog Box Keys
Editing Keys
Help Keys
Menu Keys
System Keys
Text Selection Keys
Windows Keys

Basic Windows Skills
Arranging Application Windows and Icons
Changing a Window's Size
Check Boxes
Choosing Menu Commands
Closing Active Windows
Closing Dialog Boxes

---

4 Move the mouse ▷ until it is over a topic (example: Windows Help Index). The ▷ turns into a ⨍. Click the mouse.

Note: This only happens over dimmed or underlined text.

■ A detailed explanation of that topic appears.

*Note: Click the **Index** button to return to the **Program Manager** Help window (2nd screen in this sequence).*

5 Move the mouse ▷ over the next topic of interest and click the mouse for more information.

Program Manager Help – PROGMAN.HLP

File   Edit   Bookmark   Help

Index   Back   Browse   Browse   Search...

Index to Windows and Program Manager Help

From the topics below, choose Program Manager Help Index to learn more about Program Manager. Or choose windows Help Index to learn about basic Windows features.

Help Indexes
Program Manager Help Index
Windows Help Index

To choose a Help Index:

Mouse   *   Point to the underlined topic you want to view and click the mouse button. When the *pointer* is over an item you can choose, the pointer changes to a hand icon.

Keyboard   *   Press Tab to move the highlight to the underlined topic you want to view, and then press Enter.

Program Manager Help – PROGMAN.HLP

File   Edit   Bookmark   Help

Index   Back   Browse   Browse   Search

Index to Windows and Program Manager Help

From the topics below, choose Program Manager Help Index to learn more about Program Manager. Or choose windows Help Index to learn about basic Windows features.

pointer

The arrow-shaped cursor on the screen that follows the mouse's movement and indicates which area of the screen will be affected when you click the mouse button. The pointer usually appears as an arrow, but changes shape during certain tasks.

A few other pointer shapes: ⇕ ✛ ⨍

When the *pointer* is over an item you can choose, the pointer changes to a hand icon.

Keyboard   *   Press Tab to move the highlight to the underlined topic you want to view, and then press Enter.

---

4 Move the mouse ▷ until it is over a term (example: pointer) and it turns into a ⨍. Click and hold down the left button.

Note: This only applies to dimmed and dotted underlined text.

■ A detailed explanation of that term appears.

SEARCH FOR A SPECIFIC WORD OR PHRASE

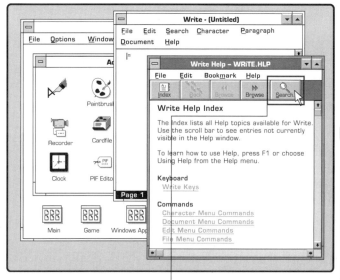

Search for help information on a word (example: copy) in an application (example: Write).

1 Start **Write** by double clicking its icon.

2 Press **F1** and the **Write Help** window appears.

3 Click the **Search** button to display the **Search** dialog box on the next screen.

4 Type the word or phrase you want help on (example: **copy**). Notice that the top entry in the List Box matches the characters you type.

or

■ Use the mouse ▷ to scroll through the **List Box** and then click on the appropriate entry.

ADD A NOTE TO A TOPIC

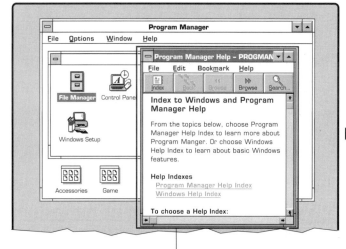

A note can be added to any Help topic to remind you of important related information.

1 Select any Help topic that you want to add a note to. For example, press **F1** to display the **Program Managers Help** window shown above.

2 Press **Alt,E,A** to display the **Help Annotation** dialog box.

3 Type in a note related to this Help topic.

4 Press **Enter** to save the note.

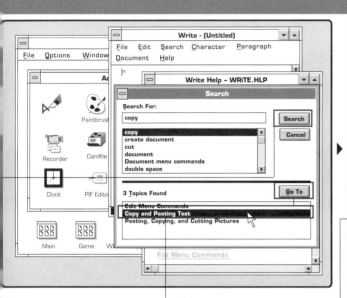

5 When the **List Box** displays the selected entry, click the **Search** button to find topics related to that entry.

6 Click a topic of interest to select it (example: **Copying and Pasting Text**). Then click the **Go To** button.

■ Help on the selected topic appears.

■ If a Help window contains hard to remember information, click its **Minimize** button to reduce it to an icon. To restore the window, double click its icon.

TO ERASE A NOTE

Press **Alt**,**E**,**A** and then click the **Delete** button.

■ A paper clip symbol appears indicating a note exists for this topic.

■ To access a note, press **Alt**,**E**,**A**.

Windows Basics

Managing Your Programs

Managing Your Directories

Create a File

Managing Your Files

Managing Your Diskettes

Help

INDEX